ORGANIZED CRIME

BLITZ EDITIONS

Published by Blitz Editions
an imprint of Bookmart Ltd
Registered Number 2372865
Trading as Bookmart Ltd
Desford Road
Enderby
Leicester LE9 5AD

ISBN 1 85605 111 0

This material has previously appeared in *Crimes and Victims*
50 938

Every effort has been made to contact the copyright holders for the pictures.
In some cases they have been untraceable, for which we offer our apologies.
Thanks to the following libraries and picture agencies which supplied pictures:

Associated Press, AP Worldwide, AGIP, Black Museum, Culver Pictures,
Mary Evans Photo Library, Jack Hickes Photography, Fairfax Ltd,
Illustrated London News, Hulton-Deutsch Collection, News Ltd of Australia,
Popperfotos, Press Association, Rex Features, Frank Spooner Pictures,
Syndication International, Suddeutscher Verlag, Topham, UPI/Bettmann

The Author
J. Anderson Black is a fine arts graduate from Edinburgh University.
He has been a professional writer for more than twenty-five years,
and his published work covers a wide range of topics from art to crime,
as well as three novels and several screenplays for feature films.

ORGANIZED CRIME

THE KRAY TWINS
A Lethal Double-Act

From playground bullies via the boxing ring, East End twins Reggie and Ronnie Kray went on to build a gangland empire the like of which London had never seen before. 'The Firm' allowed no liberties to be taken, and was feared by all

Above: ***'I gotta horse!' Ronnie Kray, with minder, poses briefly as a racehorse owner.***

On 24 October 1933 twin boys were born to Mrs Violet Kray of 178 Vallance Road, Bethnal Green. She named them Reginald and Ronald.

The twins grew up in London's East End, surrounded by street traders, boxers and petty criminals. Fighting was a way of life for children in Bethnal Green. But Reggie and Ronnie seemed to derive enormous pleasure out of terrifying and hurting other human beings.

BOXERS

At fourteen they found another, more acceptable outlet for their violent tendencies – boxing.

Both lads showed real promise as amateurs, but demonstrated a completely different approach to the sport, a difference which was reflected in their personalities as men. Reggie was a skilful

Opposite: ***At 18 years of age, Reggie and Ronnie Kray were successful young boxers with two years of professional experience behind them. Their styles were very different, however: Reggie was a skilled fighter, but Ronnie won his matches by vicious slugging.***

Left: ***The twins were adored by their mother Vi, for whom they could do no wrong. But their career in boxing soon came to an end when they were put on probation for beating up a police constable.***

Above: ***To the end of her life Vi kept her faith in her sons. They are seen together here with the twins' grandfather, who had also been a professional boxer, outside her modest East End house in Vallance Road.***

In boxing as in life, Ronnie was a hard and fearless slugger

and resourceful boxer, whereas Ronnie was a slugger, totally fearless and vicious. The net result of these contrasting styles, however, was the same. They both won every fight.

At sixteen the twins turned professional and maintained their unbeaten record until their careers were brought to an abrupt halt. They both got into a street fight during which they beat up a police constable.

They were let off with a probationary sentence. But fight managers dislike boxers with a reputation for violence outside the ring, since any serious conviction usually costs a fighter his licence.

The next watershed in the Krays' young lives came in March 1952, when they were called up to do their National Service. They had no intention of spending two years in the Royal Fusiliers and made that immediately and absolutely clear. The boys absconded and were back at Vallance Road for tea after a mere six hours of army service.

They were arrested, escaped, arrested again and escaped again. They continued their running battle with the army for more than a year before the Royal Fusiliers gave up on them. After spending nine months in a military prison at Shepton Mallet they were given a dishonourable discharge.

MANAGEMENT PROSPECTS

When they were released in 1953, the twins went straight back to the East End.

While they considered their career prospects, the twins established semi-residence in the Regal Billiard Hall in the Mile End Road. It was a seedy, down-at-heel place which had become a popular hang-out for small-time criminals.

Around the time the Krays arrived at the Regal, there was a sudden outbreak of violence and vandalism. The twins never seemed to be directly involved, but there were fights every night, and there were anonymous threats to burn the place down.

The manager eventually left and the twins approached the owners with an offer. They would pay the owners £5 a week to take the hall over. The owners accepted, the Krays became managers, and the violence and vandalism stopped as abruptly as it had started.

Reggie, who proved an astute businessman, set about renovating and redecorating the Regal, and before long it was becoming a successful commercial concern.

It also continued to serve as a meeting point for local criminals, but now the Krays offered them a genuine service. There were lock-up cubicles under the seats for thieves' tools, and stolen goods could be stashed round the back. The Krays received a cut of every job planned or executed from their premises.

The billiard hall was now making good money, and the Krays were supplementing this with extortion. Clubs, billiard halls, unlicensed gambling dens and illicit bookmakers from Bethnal Green and Mile End were soon paying a 'pension' to 'the Firm', as the Kray gang was now known.

Despite their growing reputation, however, the Krays still had no real power. Each section of the East End had its own 'guv'nor', and the twins hadn't yet achieved 'guv'nor' status.

However, their activities were causing some displeasure with these established gang bosses. There were a number of bloody showdowns and, despite being outnumbered and outgunned by their rivals, the twins always seemed to come out on top.

Above: ***From the Regal Billiard Hall in London's Mile End Road, the Kray twins soon moved on to bigger and better enterprises. At a charity evening in the Kentucky Club, they line up for a photograph with brother Charles (behind Ronnie, right).***

Right: ***The psychopathic Ronnie was a practising homosexual, but Reggie did not resemble his twin brother in this respect. Here he escorts long-standing girl-friend Frances Shea in Vallance Road.***

ASPIRATION 'UP WEST'

By 1955, the Firm was the established power through Hackney and Mile End to Walthamstow. And they were starting to make real money.

But the twins had their sights set on bigger things. Reggie wanted the 'good life', the wealth that West End crime offered, and Ronnie craved the kudos that came with being a big-time gangland boss.

Ronnie spent most of his time planning elaborate deals and alliances which would establish the Firm 'up West', but none of them ever quite worked out. The Krays were too wild and too dangerous for the established West End gangs to deal with. They closed ranks and shut the twins out.

This frustrated Ronnie, and the more frustrated he became, the more violent his thinking became. He grew increasingly paranoid and psychotic, toting his guns in public and threatening to 'do' people all the time.

Ronnie finally had his chance to use his gun for real when a young docker tried to cheat one of the Firm's associates. The docker gave Ronnie some lip, and Ronnie promptly shot him in the leg.

Everyone in the East End, including

the police, knew that the Firm were responsible for the shooting, and after a few hours they picked up a man they believed to be Ronnie Kray and put him into an identification parade.

'Yes, but I'm not Ronald Kray,' said the man in the line-up. 'I'm Reggie Kray. I can prove it – and, what's more, I can prove I wasn't anywhere near where this bloke says he was shot.' The police, angry and embarrassed, had no option but to free Reggie with an apology.

OUT FOR REVENGE

The police, who do not like to be bested, now had it in for the Krays. Their chance to nail one of them came the following year, in 1956.

Terry Martin, a street trader from Stepney, had been taking 'extreme liberties', and Ronnie decided that he needed 'teaching a lesson'. He dragged Martin out of the Britannia pub in Watney Street, slashed him twice on the head with a bayonet, stabbed him in the shoulder and then kicked him unconscious.

Ronnie was being driven home in his new black Buick when police picked him up. They found a crowbar and a bayonet in the car and when they asked how he got blood on his shirt, Ronnie shrugged. 'I 'ad a nose bleed, di'n' I?'

Ronnie was found guilty of grievous bodily harm and sentenced to three years' imprisonment.

It was the first time since they were born that the twins had been separated for more than a few days at a time, and most East End pundits said it would be the end of the Firm.

They were wrong. Reggie, freed from his brother's manic influence, not only continued to run the gang's illegal activities but also embarked on several legitimate enterprises. He rented an empty shop in Bow Road with his older brother Charles and converted it into a drinking club, the Double R – in honour of himself and his absent brother.

The club was a huge success, not only

Above: ***Reggie eventually married Frances Shea. He looks on as best man Ronnie kisses the bride.***

DESPITE THE BAYONET FOUND IN HIS CAR, RONNIE CASUALLY TOLD THE POLICE HIS BLOODSTAINED SHIRT WAS CAUSED BY A NOSE BLEED

Left: ***Bride and groom and best man pose for the camera at the wedding reception.***

Right: ***All for one and one for all: the twins and brother Charles affirm their family ties.***

with local villains but also with certain members of the entertainment and sporting fraternities who considered it was chic to rub shoulders with the criminal element.

INSANITY

In prison, Ronnie Kray soon showed signs of severe mental illness. He became paranoid and depressed and complained of 'hearing voices'. He couldn't sleep, and wouldn't eat because he was convinced that he was being poisoned.

He was transferred to the psychiatric wing of Winchester Prison for observation. There he was put on sedatives and showed some signs of improvement until the morning he received news that his favourite auntie, Rose, had died of cancer.

By that evening Ronnie was totally incoherent and had to be strapped into a straitjacket for his own protection. The following day, doctors at Winchester certified Ronald Kray as legally insane.

Ronnie was transferred to Long Grove Hospital near Epsom where he received the very best psychiatric treatment. He was diagnosed as a paranoid schizophrenic.

Doctors treated his illness with a new wonder drug called Stematol. Within days Ronnie was stabilized and was showing marked signs of improvement.

But he was still technically insane which meant that, despite the fact that he had only a year of his sentence to serve, the authorities could detain him indefinitely.

Alarmed by this prospect, Reggie Kray decided something had to be done to rectify the situation. He drove up to Long Grove, switched clothes with his brother and took his place in the hospital while Ronnie walked to freedom.

On the run, Ronnie was taken to see a top Harley Street psychiatrist who, not knowing his patient's true identity, pronounced him sane.

But Ronald Kray was most certainly not sane. Without close medical supervision, his condition deteriorated rapidly. Even Reggie was eventually forced to face the fact that his brother needed professional help. So he did the unthinkable. He called the police.

Above: ***Although Reggie was cleverer and more responsible than his brother, he was constantly influenced by Ronnie, dressing like him and following him in his pose as a big-time gangster.***

RONNIE KRAY, IN COMMON WITH HIS HERO AL CAPONE AND THE BOSTON STRANGLER, WAS A PARANOID SCHIZOPHRENIC

Ronnie was returned not to hospital, but to jail to complete his sentence. He was no longer technically insane, so the ploy had worked. He was released in the spring of 1959.

CLEVER BUSINESS MOVES

During Ronnie's absence, Reggie and Charles Kray had proved extremely shrewd. They had moved away from street violence and consolidated their section of the East End by negotiation, albeit with underlying menace. They had also formed a loose partnership with one of the big-time West End bosses, Billy Hill. Hill had recently gone into semi-retirement but retained extensive interests in the West End, particularly illicit gambling, and he had needed someone to look after the show.

In the mid-fifties, gambling fever had hit London. Illegal casinos had become a major industry which was almost completely controlled by the underworld. Even high-society 'chemin de fer' parties at their secret Belgravia and Mayfair addresses were paying a 'fee' to the Mob to ensure that their sport continued uninterrupted.

Hill had introduced Reggie and Charles Kray to several of these parties where they acted as minders. It was a good source of income and, more important, it gave them contacts and a presence in the West End.

Parliament was on the verge of legalizing gambling, a move which was intended to legitimize the industry and to remove the criminal element from it. Reggie Kray, however, reckoned it would be just like Las Vegas – a licence to print money.

The casinos would have to be run by someone, and who better than the men who already knew the ropes, men like Reggie Kray? All he had to do was keep his nose clean and grab the opportunity when it came along. The only problem was Ronnie. He was now back on the scene, paranoid and hostile, toting guns and talking about 'doing' people.

Ironically, it was Ronnie's thuggery that eventually got the Krays their first solid stake in the West End. He had been putting pressure on racketeer landlord Peter Rachman to pay protection.

Rachman was too clever to let himself get on that particular treadmill, but knew he would have to do something to get Ronnie off his back. So he negotiated a deal which gave the Krays an interest in Esmerelda's Barn, a newly licensed casino in Belgravia's Wilton Place.

In addition to this, the Krays established themselves as 'security consultants' to other casinos in Mayfair, Chelsea and Knightsbridge, some thirty in all, each paying £150 a week for the benefit of the Firm's expertise.

By 1962, the American Mafia had started to buy stakes in some of the smarter casinos and the Krays established themselves as the Mob's London minders.

Despite Ronnie's ongoing lunacy, Reggie continued with his efforts to smarten up the Krays' image. He opened a new, plusher club in the East End, and became actively involved in a whole range of charitable works – old folks' homes, cancer appeals and boys' clubs.

By this time a certain policeman, Detective Inspector Leonard 'Nipper' Read was starting to take an unhealthy interest in the Kray twins and their Firm.

Below and bottom: ***As the twins' influence grew 'up West', so did their ambition to rub shoulders with showbiz personalities such as film star Judy Garland or actress Barbara Windsor.***

LAUNDRYMEN TO THE MOB

By 1965, business was booming for the twins. They had their casinos and clubs and their protection racket, and they were involved in large-scale fraud.

Then, in April, they were approached by one of their American Mafia contacts, Angelo Bruno, to launder $55,000 worth of stolen bearer bonds. They were part of a $2 million consignment of bonds that the Mafia was holding in New York. If the Krays did well, they could act as the exclusive Mafia fence in London.

Above: ***An unlikely pairing. The homosexual Ronnie in conversation with Christine Keeler, central character in the sex-and-security scandal involving War Minister John Profumo and Russian spy Ivanov in 1963.***

The whole idea appealed to the Firm – particularly to Ronnie, whose dream of being a big-time Mob boss seemed finally to be becoming a reality. The Firm bought the first shipment of bonds at a quarter of their face value and found, with the help of a crooked merchant banker, Alan Cooper, no trouble in disposing of them. Things had never looked better.

ORGY OF VIOLENCE

But soon people started 'taking liberties' again, and Ronnie couldn't stand for that. The target of his displeasure on this occasion was one George Cornell, an enforcer for the rival Richardson gang.

On 9 March 1966, Ronnie slipped his 9mm Mauser automatic into his shoulder holster, collected henchman Ian Barrie, and told 'Scotch' Jack Dickson to drive them down to one of Cornell's hangouts, a pub called the Blind Begger.

When they arrived, Cornell was sitting perched on a stool at the far end of the bar, drinking a beer with a couple of friends.

'Well, look who's here!' said Cornell, smiling. But his smile soon evaporated as Barrie fired two warning shots into the ceiling. Ronnie Kray never spoke. He raised his Mauser and shot Cornell through the head. The massive 9mm shell exploded his skull and he died instantly.

When the police arrived at the Blind Begger, nobody had seen anything. The identity of George Cornell's killer, however, was the worst-kept secret in the East End. And among those who were fully aware of his identity was Detective Inspector 'Nipper' Read.

IN THE EARLY SIXTIES THE KRAYS MADE THEIR FIRST CONTACTS WITH THE US MAFIA - WHICH WOULD PROVE VERY USEFUL LATER

JACK 'THE HAT' MCVITIE HAD DONE MUCH TO IRK THE TWINS, BUT HIS ONE SUICIDAL ERROR WAS TO CALL RONNIE A 'FAT POOF'

Rather than lying low after the murder of Cornell, Ronnie seemed to have his taste for violence heightened and he embarked on an orgy of maiming and killing.

All reason seemed to leave the twins at this point in time. Perhaps their most bizarre escapade involved Frank 'Mad Axe Man' Mitchell.

Mitchell, an old friend of Ronnie's, was serving a thirty-two-year sentence in Dartmoor for robbery with violence.

On 12 December 1966 they had him snatched from a working party on the moor. A massive manhunt ensued and the Krays hid Mitchell in a friend's flat in Barking. But it wasn't long before the twins regretted taking Mitchell on. His incessant, child-like demands on them became intolerable. He, too, would have to be taught a lesson.

On Christmas Eve, Reggie Kray told Mitchell that he was going to be moved down to a safe house for the holiday. At 8.30 p.m., he was bundled into the back of a van which sped off down Barking Road. Frank Mitchell was never seen again.

THE KILLING OF JACK 'THE HAT'

The Firm was falling apart at the seams, but desertion from the ranks was rare. Deemed a 'diabolical liberty', it was dealt with appropriately.

One exception was Jack 'The Hat' McVitie, a strong-arm man who had worked with the Krays at various times over the years. He was definitely a liberty-taker. He had taken money from Reggie for a contract killing and then bungled it. He had threatened the twins behind their back. And, worst of all, he had described Ronnie as a 'fat poof'.

The twins agreed that McVitie must be punished. At Ronnie's insistence, Reggie would be the one to mete out that punishment.

McVitie was lured to a basement flat in Stoke Newington with the promise of a lively party. Arriving at the flat just before midnight, he demanded: 'Where's all the birds and all the booze?'

As Ronnie Kray got up to greet him from the sofa, Reggie stepped out from behind the door, aimed a .32 automatic at McVitie's head and pulled the trigger.

The gun jammed and Reggie threw himself at his hapless victim. Ronnie watched the ensuing struggle, egging his brother on with hysterical screams. McVitie broke free and dived through a window, but Reggie caught his legs and dragged him back into the room and plunged a carving knife into his face, chest and stomach. He slid on to the floor and died in an ocean of his own blood.

Like Mitchell and the others, McVitie's body was spirited away and never found. But again the East End underworld and the police, notably Detective Inspector 'Nipper' Read, were well aware of what had happened and who was responsible.

Above: ***After the murder of George Cornell the Kray twins were held for questioning by the police for 36 hours, before returning to Vallance Road to give an informal press conference.***

GUNNING FOR THE TWINS

'Nipper' Read was a textbook detective. Hard-working, methodical and totally dedicated, he was a five-foot-seven terrier who had his teeth into the Krays and wasn't about to let go.

After the McVitie murder Read was assigned a team of fourteen detectives and set up an undercover operation in an anonymous block of government offices south of the Thames. Their sole task was to build a case against the Kray twins.

Read knew that any attempt to convict the Krays of a specific crime was doomed to failure. They were too powerful and too well organized. They could intimidate witnesses and threaten jurors. They had the money to retain top lawyers and pay others to take the blame or provide them with an alibi.

'I HATE THE SIGHT OF BLOOD,' SAID ONE MAN WHO REFUSED TO TESTIFY AGAINST THE KRAYS. 'PARTICULARLY MY OWN'

Left: ***Reggie leaves the Central Criminal Court (the 'Old Bailey') in 1965, after successfully evading charges of extortion with menaces.***

No – if Read was to get them, he would have to persuade one or more of their past victims to testify against them.

Read made a list of thirty people whom the Krays had maimed or robbed over the past decade. Then he and his team went about the laborious process of questioning them all.

As well as making countless enquiries in London, detectives travelled to Scotland, Canada, Belgium, Spain and the United States.

They were met with a wall of silence. The reason for people's reticence was not hard to understand. In the words of one potential witness whom the Krays had maimed and ruined, but was reluctant to talk: 'I hate the sight of blood, particularly my own.'

Evidence might have been slow in materializing, but 'Nipper' Read and his team did start to accumulate information, first from Leslie Payne, the Krays' erstwhile business manager, and later from Alan Cooper, the merchant banker who had fenced the Mafia's bearer bonds.

The police were gradually building up a complete picture of the Firm's activities. But they still didn't have any hard evidence which they could take in front of a jury.

Six months passed and the investigation had stalled. Read, however, felt confident that, if the Krays and their associates were all safely behind bars, reluctant witnesses would summon up the

Above: ***The picture of innocence, Ronnie and Reggie sip tea while answering journalists' questions after their 36-hour detention.***

courage to come forward.

He would have to arrest and charge the Krays before he had finished preparing his case. It was a massive gamble, but Read was rapidly running out of options.

At 6a.m. on 9 May 1968, sixty police officers descended on twenty-four separate addresses across London. 'Nipper' Read had his revolver drawn as his men broke down the door of Braithwaite House, where the twins each had a flat.

He needn't have worried. Both men were sound asleep, Reggie with a girl from Walthamstow, Ronnie with a fair-haired teenage boy from Bethnal Green.

FIGHT TO THE FINISH

The twins were charged with murder, extortion and sundry other offences, and were remanded in Brixton Jail.

Read had only a few weeks before the preliminary hearings in which to persuade witnesses to talk and thereby clinch his case. His job wasn't made any easier by the fact that two of the firm, Ronnie Hart and Ian Barrie were still on the loose.

Because the twins were still on remand and technically innocent, they were allowed as many visitors as they wanted. It was therefore easy for them to pass messages to their fugitive henchmen, who in turn could continue to intimidate witnesses.

So Read went all out to get the two men. Hart was the first to be caught. The police found him hiding in a caravan with his girlfriend. He gave them no trouble and confessed to everything.

Three days later they picked up Barrie in Mile End. He was drunk, broke and frightened. He, too, told the police everything they wanted to know.

With the threat of a Kray reprisal force removed, the whole situation changed. Conmen, club owners and racketeers suddenly got their memories back. When the trial opened on 6 July, long-forgotten victims, accomplices saving their own skins, and eye-witnesses all trooped through the witness box.

The death blow for the Krays came, however, with the appearance of the barmaid from the Blind Beggar. Previously she had been too frightened to identify Ronnie after the shooting of George Cornell. Now she said she was absolutely certain that it had been Ronnie Kray who had fired the fatal shot.

The defence made a brave attempt at discrediting the witnesses, but the barmaid's story stuck, and the Krays were effectively finished.

The twins were arrogant and defiant throughout the long trial, but even they must have realized that the verdict was a foregone conclusion. They were found guilty of the murders of Cornell and McVitie and sentenced to life imprisonment, '...which,' Mr Justice Melford Stevenson said, 'I recommend should not be less than thirty years.' If his wishes were respected, the Kray twins would be sixty-four before they were released.

It would be easy to write off Reggie and Ronnie Kray as a couple of vicious East End thugs. They certainly were that, but they were much more besides. They were professionals of violence who operated on a scale previously unknown in Britain.

The odds against their rise to power were enormous. They were both mentally unstable and had no education or finesse. Yet they came closer to building a crime empire on the lines of Al Capone than any other criminal organization that London has ever known. They were truly dangerous men on the grand scale.

AL CAPONE
Public Enemy No. One

Neither a Mafioso nor even a Sicilian, by the age of twenty-six Al Capone had connived and murdered his way to become the biggest gangland boss in the most lawless city in America. But what was the truth and how much was legend?

For most people the very mention of organized crime conjures up a whole range of vivid images – the roaring twenties, Chicago, bootleg whiskey, speakeasies and, of course, Al Capone.

It is not that Chicago, or even America, ever had a monopoly on organized crime, it is merely the very public nature of its criminals which is so evocative. Gangsters with colourful nicknames like 'Pretty Boy' Floyd, 'Legs' Diamond, 'Machine Gun' Jack McGurn and Al 'Scarface' Capone, captured the public imagination and became a part of criminal folklore.

THE YOUNG BROOKLYN IMMIGRANT

Contrary to popular myth, Al Capone was never a member of the Mafia. He wasn't even a Sicilian. He hated Sicilians and spent most of his active years at loggerheads with various branches of the Mob. Capone was a gangster pure and simple, a racketeer whose only loyalty was to himself and his immediate family.

Born in Brooklyn in 1899, Alphonse was the fourth son of Gabriele and Teresa Capone, a Neapolitan couple who had emigrated from Italy some six years earlier. As a teenager, Al ran with the

Opposite: ***From a flashy teenage thug, Capone rapidly grew into a portly, conservatively-dressed figure who could have been taken for a successful middle-aged businessman.***

Below: ***Capone's career as a big-time mobster lasted a mere six years, but in that time he acquired all the trappings and habits of a rich man.***

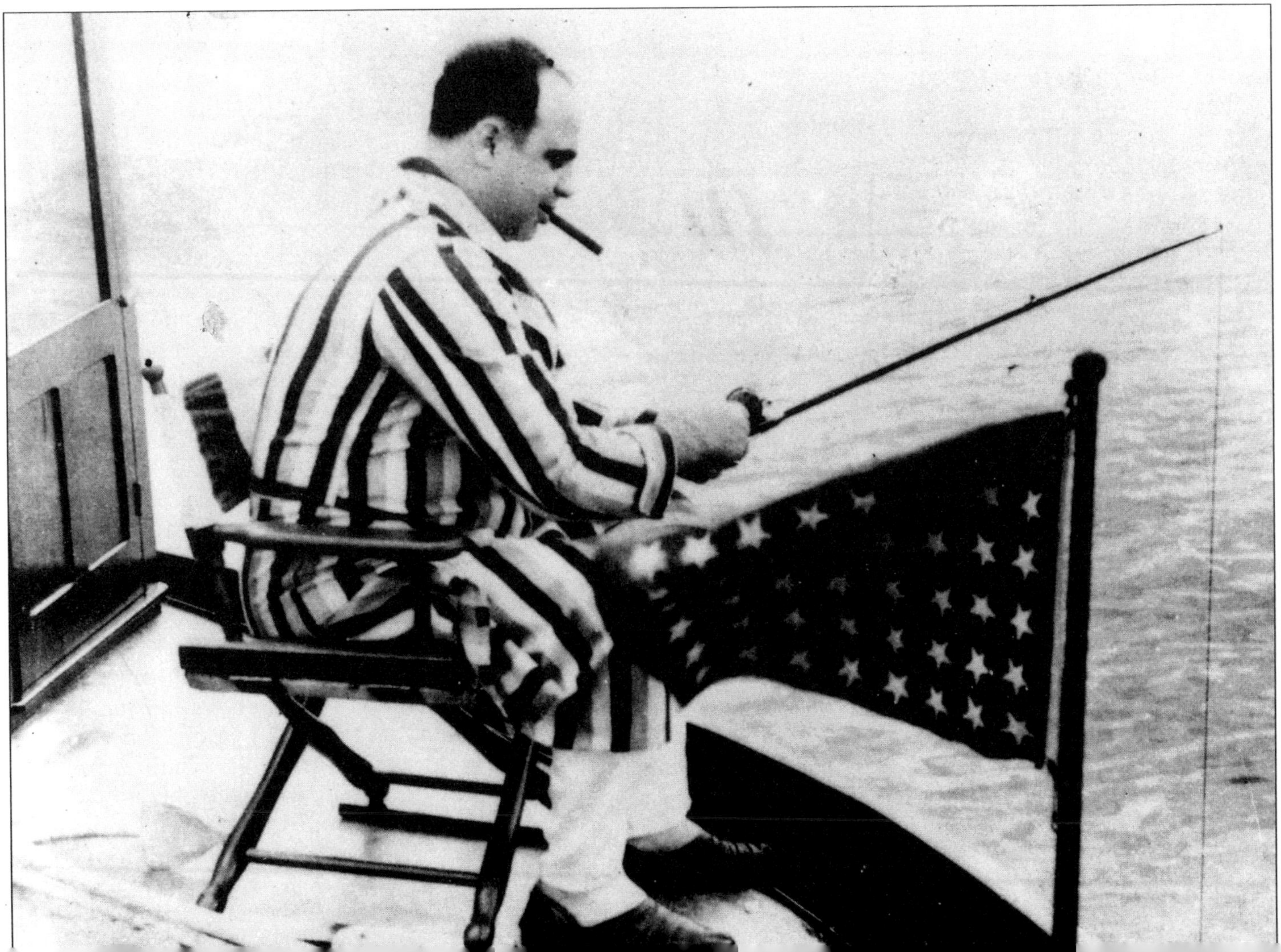

murderous Five Points gang which was led by fellow-Italian and partner-to-be John Torrio.

He had his first brush with the Mafia when he was fifteen. The Black Hand, a Mafia murder squad, had been extorting money from his father. Capone hunted down the two men responsible and shot them dead. Torrio was impressed by the young man's nerve and ruthless efficiency. Six years later, in 1919, when Torrio was in the process of building his bootlegging empire in Chicago, he remembered the name of Al Capone.

Torrio had been in Chicago for about five years when the Volsted Act was passed and America went dry. The country developed an immediate and insatiable thirst which organized crime was ready and willing to slake. In Chicago, drinkers were supplied by one of a dozen big gangs, each with its own clearly defined territory.

Torrio's gang controlled the South Side of the city and soon teamed up with the Irish Druggan-Lake gang who supplied the inner West Side. The North Side of Chicago was the territory of Dion O'Banion, a florist and failed safe-cracker, who had a flower shop opposite the Holy Name Cathedral.

O'Banion could have made a legitimate income by supplying floral tributes to the victims of gangland slayings. Instead he teamed up with two Polish Catholics, George 'Bugs' Moran and Hymie Weiss. Together, these three were the biggest challenge to Torrio's pre-eminence in the city.

The other important gang were the Gennas who controlled the West Side. These six brothers from Marsala in Sicily were the most ruthless of all the Chicago gangsters; they didn't only kill for gain and self-protection – they killed for fun.

In the first year of Prohibition, there was comparatively little trouble between the rival gangs. There was more than enough business for everyone, and most of the gangsters' energy was devoted to maintaining supply to meet the enormous demand.

By 1920, however, things were getting better organized and some of the smaller gangs were looking to expand their territories. The O'Donnell gang from the South Side started hijacking Torrio's beer trucks and smashing up his speakeasies. Torrio retaliated by killing several of O'Donnell's drivers. Elsewhere in the city, other gangs were at each others' throats.

Torrio could see the way things were going and decided that, if he was to fulfil his ambition and have overall control of Chicago, he would need to import some extra muscle. So he called up Al Capone, now twenty-one and a lieutenant in the Five Points gang, and made him an offer he couldn't refuse: 25 per cent of existing turnover and 50 per cent of all new business.

In the early days of the partnership Capone did the killing for both himself and Torrio. One of his first victims was a small-time crook called Joe Howard. Howard had ideas above his station and one night hijacked two of Torrio's booze trucks. The following evening, Joe was having a drink in his neighbourhood bar. Capone walked in with a broad grin on his face. It was happy hour.

Above: ***Chicago was no place to bring up his children, said Capone, and in 1928, after an unsuccessful attempt to settle in California, he purchased a magnificent house on Palm Island, Miami.***

IMPRESSED BY THE TEENAGE CAPONE'S STYLE, WHEN GANG LEADER TORRIO STARTED BOOTLEGGING HE TOOK HIM ON AS A PARTNER

'Hi, Al,' Joe said, sticking out his hand. Capone fired six shots into his body at point-blank range, and Howard fell to the bar-room floor with a smile of welcome still on his face. The police immediately put out an arrest warrant on Capone, but had to release him when all the eye-witnesses developed amnesia.

By the end of 1923, Capone had gained control of the middle-class Chicago suburb of Cicero and made it his personal headquarters. By a combination of bribery and intimidation, he had the entire administration in his pocket – mayor, town clerk and town attorney. So backed, he was free to do whatever he liked. His illegal casinos and brothels and bars were open day and night.

By this time Torrio and Capone were each making in excess of $100,000 a week, but they were still a long way from gaining absolute control of the city. The O'Banion gang and the Gennas still controlled the North and West sides. Capone was in favour of all-out war to eliminate the competition; Torrio preferred to sit back and pick his moment.

CAPONE WALKED INTO THE BAR AND FIRED SIX SHOTS INTO HOWARD AT CLOSE RANGE. IT WAS HAPPY HOUR

BENEATH GANGLAND CHIEF O'BANION'S FUNERAL CASKET WAS THE INSCRIPTION: 'SUFFER THE LITTLE CHILDREN TO COME UNTO ME'

In late October 1924, the O'Banion gang hijacked a large shipment of the Gennas' Canadian whiskey. They swore revenge. 'To hell with them Sicilians,' O'Banion said to reporters. A war was in the offing and this was just the situation Torrio and Capone had been waiting for.

WAR BREAKS OUT IN CHICAGO

On 4 November O'Banion was in the back room of his florist's when he heard someone come into the shop. He went out to welcome three customers.

Six shots rang out, the last of which exploded into O'Banion's left cheek. He sprawled back into his flower display as his assassins made good their escape. When the police arrived at the shop, Dion O'Banion was dead.

Torrio, Capone and the Genna brothers were all questioned by the police, but all had satisfactory explanations as to their whereabouts at the time of the killing. The street outside O'Banion's shop had been crowded, yet no one had seen anything. Faced with the customary wall of silence, the coroner was forced to bring in a finding of 'unlawful killing at the hands of a person or persons unknown'.

The tradition of lavish funerals for American gangsters started with O'Banion. His body lay 'in state' at the undertaker's for three days. A contemporary report describes the scene: 'Silver angels stood at the head and feet with their heads bowed in the light of ten candles that burned in solid golden candlesticks they held in their hands. Beneath the casket, on a marble slab that supports its glory, is the inscription: "Suffer the little children to come unto me." And over it all the perfume of flowers.'

At the funeral, mounted police kept order as the cortege of gangsters rolled slowly through the streets of Chicago, followed by twenty-six trucks of flowers, valued at more than $50,000. Among the floral tributes was a basket of red roses with a card which read, 'From Al'.

Both Capone and Torrio solemnly attended the funeral, but no one was fooled – least of all Hymie Weiss, O'Banion's most trusted lieutenant and the new boss of his organization. Weiss was a cold-blooded killer who had devised a method of assassination in which the victim was seated in the front passenger seat of the car with his killer directly behind him. He was then shot in the back of the head. After such a murder, Weiss would calmly say that his victim had been 'taken for a ride'. And so the expression became part of modern parlance.

Weiss, who was genuinely heartbroken by O'Banion's death – observers described him as crying like a baby, swore to get his revenge. Days later Capone's car was machine-gunned. Al escaped unhurt, but two weeks later John Torrio was gunned down in front of his wife by another O'Banion man, Bugs Moran.

Torrio recovered from his wounds, but only weeks later he was jailed for nine months for operating a brewery. Badly shaken by Moran's attack, he had steel screens fitted to the windows of his cell and hired three extra deputy sheriffs to stand sentry.

On his release in October 1925, he announced that he was leaving Chicago, which he described as being 'too violent'. The fact is, at the age of forty-eight, Johnnie Torrio had lost his nerve. This was a game for young men, and the young man on the spot was Al Capone.

THE KING IS DEAD – LONG LIVE THE KING!

So, at the age of 26, Al Capone inherited the entire Torrio empire. His promotion to unrivalled boss of Chicago was helped by the demise of the six Genna brothers. Angelo, Mike and Antonio were killed in separate gun battles within the space of six weeks. The three surviving brothers fled to their home town of Marsala in Sicily. While there is no evidence to connect Capone with the killings, he made no secret of his pleasure at the Gennas' departure.

The Sicilians might have been out of the way, but Hymie Weiss wasn't finished yet. His second attempt on Capone's life was anything but subtle, and highlighted the level of lawlessness that existed in Chicago in 1925. In broad daylight, eight carloads of gunmen made an assault on Capone's Cicero headquarters, the Hawthorne Inn, firing more than a thousand rounds into the building in a matter of seconds.

Again Capone escaped unscathed and, with customary largesse, paid $10,000 out of his own pocket to save the sight of a woman who had been injured in the cross-fire. Capone had overlooked the first attempt on his life by the North Side

Above and right: ***14 February 1929. At 10.30 a.m., while Al established an alibi in Miami, six members of Bugs Moran's gang were shot down in a Chicago garage by Capone's men disguised as policemen.***

gang, considering it legitimate revenge for the killing of their boss Dion O'Banion. Now he had had enough.

On 11 October 1926, Weiss was machine-gunned to death on the steps of Holy Name Cathedral.

Now only Bugs Moran was left alive to challenge Capone's absolute control of Chicago. And Moran could wait. Ten days after the execution of Weiss, Capone chaired a meeting of Chicago gang bosses to negotiate a peaceful division of Cook County: 'We're a bunch of saps to be killing each other,' he postulated.

For a while after that the peace held and there were no gangland slayings. Everyone was making a fortune, and none more than Al Capone. His turnover was truly astonishing. In Cook County he controlled ten thousand speakeasies, each purchasing an average of six barrels of beer a week costing a total of $3.5 million. In addition they were each buying two cases of liquor at $90, making another $1.8 million. (Beer was costing Capone about $5 a barrel to make, and liquor about $20 a case.) Added to all this, Capone had his other rackets – gambling and vice – which contributed to a grand total of about $6.5 million per week.

He had huge overheads, of course, not least of which was his illicit payroll. Everyone was on the take in Chicago, from humble patrolmen to the city's mayor 'Big Bill' Thompson, whose 1927 re-election campaign Capone financed to the tune of $260,000. It is estimated that his annual graft bill to the police, judges and politicians came to more than $30 million.

Capone was no longer the flashy, loud-mouthed thug that arrived in Chicago in 1919. He was now an immaculately tailored, even conservative figure, sporting hand-made silk shirts and solitaire diamond tie-pins. Despite the fact that he was still only twenty-six, he gave the impression of being a successful, middle-aged businessman.

Capone's public image was important to him, and he was given to ostentatious displays of generosity. He paid for church roofs to be restored; he gave $10,000 to Pennsylvania's striking miners and,

Above: ***When Herbert Hoover was elected President of the United States in 1929, he named Capone as his prime target in an attack on lawlessness. The mobster was finally indicted on a charge of income tax evasion. Here seated with his lawyers, he looks confident of a successful outcome to the hearing.***

during the Depression, he opened a string of soup kitchens and contributed more than $2 million of his own money to help down-and-outs.

Everyone in Chicago knew that Al Capone was a bootlegger, and most of them didn't care. To the vast majority of ordinary people Prohibition was a nonsense anyway, so bootlegging wasn't a real crime. He had become a success story, a working-class hero.

THE ST VALENTINE'S DAY MASSACRE

By 1928 Al Capone felt secure enough about his hold on Chicago to spend time away from the city. He was a devoted family man, who wanted his dependants to benefit from his vast wealth. Chicago was no place to bring up children, he said, and so he set about looking for a suitable second home away from the turmoil of the big city.

He quite liked the look of California, but California didn't like the look of him and summarily booted him out. Next he tried Florida and, despite the violent objections of honest citizens, managed to procure a magnificent house on Palm Island, Miami.

Capone spent Christmas and the New Year of 1929 in his new home. He had a lot to be thankful for. He was not yet thirty, had amassed a vast fortune and was the undisputed boss of America's second city. Unfortunately for Capone, one man didn't quite see it like that.

Bugs Moran had neither forgotten nor forgiven the murder of his two associates Dion O'Banion and Hymie Weiss. He decided to take advantage of Capone's absence to make him pay. With his North Side gang Moran regularly hijacked Capone's liquor shipments and then started to move in on some of his other legitimate businesses, notably dog racing and dry cleaning.

Capone may have been in Florida, but his finger was very much on the pulse. He heard all about Moran's activities and decided that they had to stop. Over the telephone he instructed Jake Guzik, his most trusted aide in Chicago, to 'take care' of Moran. The time and method of execution were discussed in minute detail, and on 14 February 1929 Capone made a point of keeping an appointment in Miami with a city official. He wanted a watertight alibi for that particular Valentine's Day.

At 10.30 a.m., as Al Capone was trying to explain to the Miami official where he had got the money to buy his Palm Island home, six of Moran's men were waiting for a truckload of hijacked whiskey in a garage on Chicago's North Clark Street. They were Frank and Peter Gusenberg, Moran's top executioners; James Clark, a Sioux Indian and Moran's brother-in-law; Al Weinshank, his accountant; Adam Heyer, his business manager; and Johnny May, a burglar and safe cracker. There was also a seventh man, whose presence has never been satisfactorily explained – an optician called Dr Richard Schwimmer. Moran himself should have been there, but had been delayed.

Shortly after 10.30 Mrs Max Landesman of 2124 North Clark Street heard shots from the garage next door. She looked out of the window and saw a man leaving the garage and getting into a large touring car. From the flat below, Miss Josephine Morin saw two men, apparently under arrest, come out of the garage with their hands up. They were followed by two uniformed police officers. All four of them got into a black Cadillac and drove off.

Mrs Landesman hurried over to the

garage, pushed open the door and saw seven men sprawled on the floor, blood streaming from their bodies. Minutes later Sergeant Tom Loftus arrived on the scene with a dozen other officers. Only one of the victims, Frank Gusenberg, was conscious, and Loftus tried to persuade him to say who had done the shootings. Gusenberg declined to comment and was shipped to hospital along with the other six victims, all of whom were pronounced dead on arrival.

Loftus maintained a vigil at Gusenberg's bedside but, true to the gangster's code of honour, he died three hours later without revealing anything.

Moran had arrived on Clark Street fifteen minutes late, and, seeing the police cars outside the garage, assumed that there had been a raid, and promptly left. Later, when he heard about the massacre, he said: 'Only Capone kills like that!'

The police were of the same opinion. So they picked up Capone's top killer, 'Machine Gun' Jack McGurn. McGurn claimed to have been with his girlfriend at the time of the killings. He was indicted for perjury, but married his girl so that the police could not force her to testify against him. Other Capone men were questioned, but soon released for lack of evidence.

In the end, no one was ever charged in connection with the St Valentine's Day massacre. But no one was in any doubt that it was carried out on the direct orders of Al Capone from the safety of his Florida retreat.

Even though Moran had survived, Capone returned to Chicago confident that he had finally crushed any opposition to his authority. Instead he found that two of his own lieutenants, John Scalise and Albert Anselmi, had been conspiring to take over the Outfit. Al invited them, along with other gang members, to a meeting at a restaurant in Hammond, Indiana. Capone was his usual jovial self until halfway through the meal, at which point he rounded on the two conspirators: 'I understand you want my job,' he said. 'Well, here it is!' and promptly clubbed them both to death with a baseball bat. It was a salutary lesson to the assembled diners.

Early in his career, Capone was known for his surgical use of violence. It was never used gratuitously – only as a tool to protect himself and to promote his business interests. This was no longer the case. Anyone who incurred his displeasure – policemen, politicians, journalists – could expect to be summarily dispatched.

'GET CAPONE!'

In March 1929, Herbert Hoover was inaugurated President of the United States. He came to office primed with a promise to tackle lawlessness in America, and he named Al Capone as his primary target.

By May of that year, Capone was feeling the heat. There were rumours of a massive contract out on his life. Some said it had been taken out by Bugs Moran, others that it was the families of Scalise and Anselmi. Whatever the truth, Capone decided it would be wise to get out of circulation for a while and, rather than going to Florida, he contrived to have himself arrested for a minor firearms offence in Philadelphia. He was expecting to get a jail sentence of thirty days, but in the event he was sent to prison for a year. Capone was initially horrified, but he soon adapted to the situation. His status was such that he was able to continue running his Chicago

WHEN BUGS MORAN HEARD ABOUT THE MASSACRE WHICH HE HAD SO NARROWLY ESCAPED, HE EXCLAIMED: 'ONLY CAPONE KILLS LIKE THAT!'

FACED WITH A 'COLONELS' REVOLT', CAPONE INVITED THE MISCREANTS TO DINNER AND THEN CLUBBED THEM TO DEATH WITH A BASEBALL BAT

Below: ***Matters are not going so well in the hearing in Chicago Federal Court in October 1931, and Capone looks grimly concerned as his financial affairs are brought out into the light.***

Right: ***The style of elaborate gangster funerals in Chicago was set by that of Dion O'Banion.***

HUNTED BY EVERY LAW AND ORDER AGENCY IN THE UNITED STATES, AL CAPONE WAS DUBBED PUBLIC ENEMY NUMBER ONE

empire from his prison cell with the minimum of inconvenience.

While Capone was in prison, the new administration in Washington were devising ways to keep him there for ever. President Hoover discussed a variety of approaches with his various agencies – the Prohibition Bureau, the Justice Department's Federal Bureau of Investigation (FBI) and the Treasury Department. Their brief was simple. Get Al Capone any way you can.

The Justice Department set about destroying Capone's booze empire by brute force. In the space of six months they raided and wrecked thirty of his breweries and seized fifty of his heavy trucks. But this was no more than an annoyance for Capone.

In Washington it was the Treasury that really took the Capone challenge on board. Their Special Intelligence Unit sent top investigator Frank Wilson to Chicago to look at Al Capone's books.

Wilson had already enjoyed spectacular success jailing gangsters who had escaped conviction for years. Among his victims were Frank Nitti, Capone's deputy; Jack Guzik, his accountant; and Capone's brother, Ralph. They had received prison terms of between eighteen months and five years. But Al Capone himself would prove tougher for Wilson than his associates.

Capone had never filed a tax return in his life. This was not a crime, so long as he did not earn more than $5000 in any given year. It was Frank Wilson's job to prove that he had. Considering Capone's lavish lifestyle, this might appear to have been a simple matter. It wasn't. Capone had no bank accounts in his own name and all his assets were listed to third parties.

Wilson and his team started a detailed probe into Capone's personal spending. They found that in the three-year period 1926-29 he had purchased more than $25,000 worth of furniture for his homes in Chicago and Florida. He had spent $7000 on suits and $40,000 on telephone calls. In all the Treasury men unearthed $165,000 worth of taxable spending. They could have gone to court with that, and they would probably have secured a conviction, which would have jailed

Capone for about three years. But that wasn't good enough. Wilson had been told to go for broke.

After months sniffing around Chicago, Wilson managed to persuade some of Capone's casino employees to turn state's evidence. Now he had Al where they wanted him. He was charged with failing to pay tax on $1 million in the years from 1925 to 1929 and, while this was a fraction of Capone's true income, it could still mean thirty years in a federal prison.

Capone's attorneys initially struck a deal with the prosecution – if Capone pleaded guilty, he would receive a sentence of not more than two and a half years. Judge Wilkerson, however, was outraged by this and threw it out. Capone withdrew his plea and elected to go to trial.

His associates immediately set about bribing or threatening members of the jury, but this was discovered and, at the very last minute, a new jury was sworn in. They heard stories of Capone's extravagant lifestyle – a lifestyle he could not possibly have supported on the $450 a month he claimed to earn – and on 24 October they returned a verdict of guilty on all charges. He was sentenced to eleven years and fined $50,000, the most severe sentence ever imposed for a tax offence.

Capone was sent to Cook County jail pending an appeal and when that failed, in May 1932, he was shipped to Atlanta Federal Penitentiary. A year later he became one of the first convicts to take up residence at Alcatraz in San Francisco Bay. He emerged from there in 1939 a physical and mental wreck. He was still only thirty-eight years old.

Capone had been diagnosed as suffering from syphilis shortly after his imprisonment in 1931. The disease had now reached its tertiary stage, and his brain was being eaten up. After his release he returned to his home on Palm Island, Florida where he lived for another seven years, increasingly mad, surrounded by his adoring family.

In 1947 he suffered a fatal brain haemorrhage. He was forty-eight years old. His body was shipped back to Chicago and buried in an elaborate mausoleum in Mount Olivet cemetery.

On his release from Alcatraz Capone was suffering from advanced syphilis which was slowly destroying his brain

Above left: ***The trial concluded, Capone is led away from Chicago Federal Court on 24 October 1931 to begin his eleven-year sentence.***

Left: ***Guarded by a US Marshall, Al Capone puts a brave face on his defeat as he is taken by train to Atlanta Federal Penitentiary.***

CARELESS THIEVES
Great Train Robbery

It was called the 'robbery of the century', yet when thieves audaciously robbed a mail train of £2.5 million they were unbelievably careless in concealing the evidence. The law was draconian, but the public secretly admired them

Shortly after 2a.m. on Thursday, 8 August 1963, the Glasgow to London mail train was nearing the end of its journey. As it passed through Leighton Buzzard in Bedfordshire, half an hour should have seen it safely into Euston. It wasn't to be, however.

A few miles further down the line, the driver, forty-eight-year-old Jack Mills, spotted an amber signal. He slowed the big diesel and prepared to stop. A mile on, at Sears Crossing, he was faced with a red light and pulled to a halt.

Mills sent his fireman, David Whitby, down the line to phone ahead for information. Within a matter of seconds, however, Mills found himself confronted by a gang of masked men clambering into his cab.

He tried to fight them off but was coshed into submission, as the biggest and most audacious robbery in history began. Half an hour later the train had been divided, moved and relieved of 128 mail sacks containing more than £2.5 million in used banknotes.

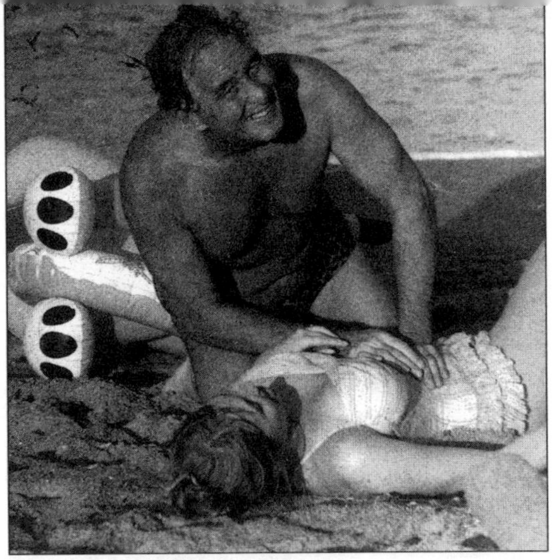

Left: *Train robber Ronald Biggs may have been a fugitive in Brazil, but he was seldom out of the public eye. In 1980 he appeared in the film* **Honeymoon** *as a swimmer who rescued German actress Dolly Dollar from drowning.*

Opposite: *Ronnie Biggs, one of the instigators of the 'robbery of the century'.*

Below: *Post Office workers lean out from the robbed train as the police start their search for clues.*

Above: ***Forensic experts inspect the Royal Mail van from which the 128 mail sacks were taken.***

THE LOCAL POLICE SOON REALIZED THAT THIS CRIME WAS TOO MAJOR FOR THEIR OWN RESOURCES, AND CALLED IN SCOTLAND YARD

FEW CLUES TO START WITH

By the time Detective Superintendent Malcolm Fewtrell, head of the Buckinghamshire CID, arrived the robbers and their spoils were long gone. Fewtrell, a seasoned professional, started routine investigative procedures, gathering physical evidence and interviewing the eighty-odd people who had been on the train.

But no one, not even Mills, Whitby or the post office sorters from whose HVP (high-value packages) coach the mail sacks had been taken, could give Fewtrell anything to go on.

It was soon obvious to Fewtrell that he was not dealing with any ordinary crime. This robbery was the work of a highly organized team, and the investigation would be on a scale far beyond the meagre resouces of his force. After consulting with his Chief Constable, he elected to 'call the Yard' – to ask for the assistance of the Metropolitan CID.

Later that day, Fewtrell attended a meeting at the headquarters of the Post Office. Present were Post Office officials including their own senior investigator, Frank Cook, and George Hatherill, deputy chief of the CID at Scotland Yard, together with a team of detectives.

Cook told the police that, in his estimation, the haul from the robbery might well be in excess of £3 million. The police for their part could give little comfort to the Post Office. All they could say for certain was that approximately fifteen men had been involved in the robbery, and that the fireman, David Whitby, had noticed an army lorry parked on the Bridego Bridge where the robbery took place.

Hatherill agreed to send two of his

Right: ***Five days after the robbery, police discovered the deserted Leatherslade farmhouse where the gang had hidden out and divided their loot.***

most able detectives – Gerald McArthur and Jack Prichard – down to Buckinghamshire to assist the local police with their enquiries. The two men returned to Aylesbury with Fewtrell that night.

The three detectives had to try and put themselves in the robbers' shoes. What would they do immediately after the robbery? A total of 128 mail sacks would not be easy to hide or transport for long distances without attracting attention.

The police decided that the robbers would hole up somewhere near the scene of the crime and distribute the money at their leisure, partly because one of the robbers had ordered the men in the HVP coach not to move for 'half an hour'. This suggested that the gang had a safe haven within half an hour's drive from the scene of the crime.

It was a guess, but they decided to back it with all their resources. Every policeman from Buckinghamshire and neighbouring forces was mobilized in a search of barges, houses and barns in a thirty-mile radius of Bridego Bridge.

So far the police were spot on. The perpetrators of the Great Train Robbery were holed up some twenty miles from Bridego Bridge at Leatherslade Farm. They had purchased it through a nominee, some weeks earlier, specifically for this purpose.

The robbery itself had gone like clockwork. The only minor hitch had been Mills, the train driver, who had offered token resistance. The haul, something over £2.5 million, had been less than they had expected. But even after they had paid their German backers a million for financing the robbery, each member of the seventeen-strong gang had received £90,000, a huge sum of money in 1963. All in all, no one was complaining.

TWO GANGS WITH COMBINED TALENTS

The robbery, which had been almost a year in the planning, was the work of not one but two London-based gangs or 'firms'. The first firm, the men who conceived the idea and did most of the ground work, consisted of Buster Edwards, Gordon Goody, Charlie Wilson, Bruce Reynolds, John Daly, Jimmy White, Ronnie Biggs and Jimmy Hussey.

They were a loose-knit team of thieves who had worked together over the years on numerous occasions with a varied degree of success.

In January 1963, Buster Edwards and Gordon Goody were approached by a friend, Brian Field, a crooked solicitor's clerk who had worked for them in the past. He claimed to have information for them about a huge shipment of cash which was theirs for the taking.

Field introduced them to an Irishman (whose name is still unknown) who told them about the high-value-package coach which made up part of the overnight mail train from Glasgow to London. It was on this coach that the banks sent all their

Above: ***Roy James, known as 'the Weasel', was arrested in December after a chase over the roof of this house in a mews in St John's Wood, north London.***

EVEN AFTER PAYING THEIR GERMAN BACKERS, THERE WAS A SMALL FORTUNE LEFT FOR DIVISION AMONG THE GANG

Above: ***In the summer of 1965, after serving little more than a year of his sentence, Ronald Biggs escaped from Wandsworth prison. More than 150 armed police surrounded Winterfold House in Surrey when told he was hiding out there, but a six-hour search revealed no trace of him.***

NORMALLY THE TRAIN CARRIED SOME SIXTY MAIL SACKS, BUT AFTER A BANK HOLIDAY THERE WERE THREE TIMES AS MANY

PANIC AND DISARRAY QUICKLY SET IN, AND THE GANG LEFT VALUABLE INFORMATION AT LEATHERSLADE FARM FOR THE POLICE TO FIND

surplus cash down to London.

Normally the coach would carry about sixty bags, the Irishman told them, but if they timed their raid to follow a bank holiday they might find upwards of two hundred, each holding about £25,000, a total haul in excess of £5 million.

Edwards and Goody were incredulous. But they assured the Irishman that if such a robbery was possible, they had the team to pull it off. They arranged a meeting with Bruce Reynolds and Charlie Wilson.

All four of them were torn between euphoria and scepticism. Before they went any further, they had to check that their informant was himself well informed.

So they staked out Euston station and saw for themselves HVP sacks being off-loaded from the night mail train. There was no doubt that the prize was there.

The only way the job could be done, they decided, was to stop the train on the track, separate the engine and the HVP coach from the main body of the train, and ransack it at their leisure. The trouble was, how do you stop a train at a predetermined spot?

Buster Edwards had a solution to the problem of stopping the train. He had heard of a south London firm, headed by one Thomas Wisbey, which had been robbing trains on the London to Brighton line for a couple of years. They had an expert who knew how to tamper with the signalling system.

Buster approached the rival gang boss and, after a period of intense haggling, terms were agreed. Wisbey would let them have his man, Roger Cordrey, as long as Wisbey himself and his partner Bob Welsh were included in the robbery as full partners.

And so the team to rob the mail train started to take shape, and the preparations began: researching a suitable location for the ambush, buying a hide-out, instructing various members of the gang in their specific tasks, and rehearsing the ambush in the most minute detail.

And now it had all paid off. The Great Train Robbers were sitting in Leatherslade Farm with more than £2.5 million in used notes.

That team of faces, already known to the police, would soon be known to the world at large. The first piece of bad news for the robbers came over the radio in the form of a public appeal by the police. They were asking for information on strange goings-on in remote dwellings, and they wanted to know about movements of army vehicles.

This presented the robbers with two problems. They had originally planned to stay at Leatherslade Farm until the

Left: ***Charlie Wilson escaped from Winson Green prison in August 1964. In January 1967 he was recaptured in Montreal, Canada, and was brought back to Britain by Detective Chief Superintendent Butler.***

Sunday night and then disperse the money using the army truck and two army Land Rovers. This was now clearly out of the question.

For the first time they were in a state of disarray and, from this point on, it was effectively every man for himself. They cleared up the farm as best they could, burning clothes and mailsacks, but in their haste to get away they were forced to leave the job half done. The various members of the gang returned to their homes and jobs in London, unaware they had left a plethora of clues for their pursuers.

THE INVESTIGATION TAKES OFF

Once the scale of the robbery was appreciated, Scotland Yard decided to beef up its support for the investigation. They brought in Chief Superintendent Tommy Butler to head up the London end. Butler would prove the downfall of many of the Train Robbers.

The first mention of Leatherslade Farm came from a cowman called John Maris on Monday, 12 August. In outbuildings the police found an army lorry and the two Land Rovers. Once inside the farm proper, half-burnt mailsacks and money wrappers left them in no doubt that they had found the hide-out.

Fewtrell and McArthur dashed to the farm. After a cursory glance they ordered that the whole area be cordoned off in readiness for the forensic team.

In London, Butler and his team had compiled a list of possible suspects to be pulled in for questioning. The bulk of the gang's names appeared on that list.

Roger Cordrey, the signals expert, was the first to be picked up. The local police found him in Bournemouth along with £141,000 in used notes, money which he found extremely difficult to explain.

The next break for the police came on Friday, 16 August. A man called John Ahern was taking a stroll in the woods near Dorking in Surrey when he came upon a briefcase, a holdall and a camelskin bag containing no less than £100,900. More important, a receipt was found made out by a German restaurant in the name of Herr and Frau Field.

Below: ***For more than five years Bruce Reynolds was a wanted man. Eventually, in November 1968, police found him in this rented house in Torquay.***

Above: *Ronald Biggs hid out in Australia, where he worked as a carpenter, until a new spate of publicity forced him to flee to Brazil. Here police search his baggage, left behind in a Melbourne motel.*

Fewtrell and McArthur knew that one Brian Field, a solicitor's clerk, had acted for several of their suspects, including Buster Edwards and Gordon Goody. They also knew that the company for which Field worked had acted in the purchase of Leatherslade Farm. They went to his home and questioned him but did not arrest him – yet.

The following day, more money – £30,440 – was found in an old caravan in the Dorking Woods by Surrey Police. Fingerprints in the caravan matched those on file for Jimmy White. At Leatherslade Farm fingerprint experts were also doing well. They had identified the prints of Charlie Wilson and Bruce Reynolds. Wilson was picked up within a few hours, but Reynolds had gone to ground .

On Thursday, 22 August local police arrested Gordon Goody in Leicester where he was having dinner with a girlfriend. They questioned him and then released him for lack of evidence.

Ronnie Biggs was next. He was pulled in on 4 September, and three days later they brought in Jim Hussey for questioning. Thomas Wisbey was questioned, released and then rearrested.

ROY JAMES WAS FINALLY ARRESTED AFTER A SPECTACULAR ROOFTOP CHASE IN LONDON

PLAYING A WAITING GAME

By the middle of September the police were fairly certain they had a complete picture of who had robbed the mail train, but Tommy Butler was in no particular hurry to find them. He reckoned that, by playing the waiting game, he stood a better chance of catching them with some of the money.

However, Butler did decide it was time to pull in Brian Field. He charged him with conspiring to rob a mail train and for being an accessory after the fact.

Police efforts were now on two fronts. The Flying Squad were trying to track down Buster Edwards, Bruce Reynolds, John Daly, Roy James and Jimmy White. The forensic team, for their part, were building up a case against them and the men already in custody, trying to tie them to the scene of the crime. It was thanks to this work that they felt confident enough to rearrest Gordon Goody on 3 October.

Over the next few weeks, Butler and his men arrested Bob Welsh and John Daly. They ran Roy James to ground in the St John's Wood area of London and, after a spectacular rooftop chase, took him into custody and charged him.

By the end of the year, nine of the sixteen men who had been at Bridego Bridge were in jail awaiting trial. Bruce Reynolds, Buster Edwards and Jimmy White were still on the run, while the other four had been overlooked or released for lack of evidence.

With no prospect of an early arrest of the three fugitives, the authorities decided to press ahead with the trial of the others.

SHOW TRIAL

The trial began on 20 January 1964. All the accused pleaded not guilty to all charges except for Roger Cordrey. He pleaded guilty to robbery and was

Right: *Chief Superintendent John Slipper and Inspector Peter Jones return to Gatwick Airport in February 1974, foiled in their attempt to repatriate Ronald Biggs.*

removed from the dock to await sentence, while the trial of the others continued.

Only Mr W. Raeburn QC, counsel for John Daly, was successful in persuading Mr Justice Davies that his client had no case to answer. Daly walked from the court a free man.

The jury returned with a verdict of guilty on all the accused.

On Wednesday, 15 April the convicted prisoners were brought to court to be sentenced. Mr Justice Edmund Davies called first for Roger John Cordrey. The judge told him that he would take into consideration Cordrey's plea of guilty and the fact that his share of the stolen money had been recovered, and would reduce his sentence accordingly. 'In respect of the four counts you must go to prison for concurrent terms of twenty years.' There was a moment's stunned silence from the court, and then a gasp. Journalists and barristers alike were astounded by the severity of the sentence. If this was Mr Justice Davies's idea of leniency, what would the others get?

One by one the guilty men faced the bench: Ronnie Biggs, thirty years; Thomas Wisbey, thirty years; Bob Welsh, Jim Hussey and Roy James, thirty years; Brian Field, twenty-five years. The convicted men were whisked off to various prisons around the country, where the true horror of their situation sank in. Even with full remission, most of them would not be released for at least twenty years.

EXPATRIATES

To the gang members still on the loose, news of the sentences was no less shattering. Any idea they may have had about turning themselves in, hoping to make a deal, evaporated. Bruce Reynolds sneaked out of the country in August 1964, Buster Edwards spent a short time in Germany having plastic surgery before leaving for Mexico City in March 1965.

In the same month that Reynolds fled to France, Charlie Wilson was sprung from Winson Green prison in Birmingham. He too was smuggled out of the country and headed for the South of France. Less than a year later, Ronnie Biggs escaped from Wandsworth and flew to Australia via Paris. By 1967 Edwards, Wilson and Reynolds had all been rearrested.

Ronnie Biggs was now the only member of the gang still at liberty. In 1969 he fled from Australia to South America, finally settling in Rio. Confident that he was finally safe – Brazil had no extradition treaty with the United Kingdom – Biggs went about making himself into an international superstar. Despite attempts to rearrest – and even to kidnap – him, he remains there to this

Above: ***Ronnie Biggs with Miss Brazil.***

BRINK'S-MAT
Robbers Strike Gold

It was almost by chance that the trio of vicious armed robbers realized they had struck gold. Their getaway van drove off groaning under the weight of three tons of bullion. Yet the biggest haul in criminal history proved harder to track down than a needle in a haystack

At 6.25 on the morning of Saturday, 26 November 1983, a group of men were gathered outside Unit 7, a warehouse on the Heathrow International Trading Estate in Hounslow, London.

Despite its unprepossessing appearance, Unit 7 is one of the world's biggest safes. It is used by Brink's-Mat, Britain's leading security company, to store hugely valuable cargoes of precious metals, currency, bonds, jewels, fine art and other high-risk consignments en-route for Heathrow International Airport.

The ground floor of the building is a huge vault containing three safes. Above this are the manager's office, a radio room, a common room and a locker room for the thirty or so guards who usually work from the building.

At precisely 6.30 Michael Scouse, the senior duty guard and 'keyman', unlocked the unit, leaving the rest of the crew outside. He switched off the alarm system, then returned to the main door. He allowed the other men to enter and locked the door again from the inside.

Scouse reset the alarms and went up to

Above: ***The police arrive at Unit 7 of the Brink's-Mat warehouse on the morning of 26 November 1983.***

Opposite: ***Even when the thieves were in prison, the police still had to track down the loot, like these bars of bullion found in Kenneth Noye's garage.***

Below: ***Police set up a mobile incident room at the scene of the Brink's-Mat robbery.***

Above: ***When Detective Constable John Fordham was stabbed to death by Kenneth Noye in January 1985, dozens of plain clothes police combed the house and grounds in the search for the missing gold.***

THE SECURITY TEAM HAD BEEN BROUGHT IN SPECIALLY FOR A BULLION RUN TO GATWICK AIRPORT

the office. He was joined by Robin Risley, the crew leader for the day. Risley knew the men had been brought in specially for a bullion run. Scouse looked through his bills of lading. 'It's gold. Three tons. Gatwick airport for the Far East via Cathay Pacific Airways. It's got to be there by 8a.m.'

Risley walked over to the common room, where the rest of the crew were warming themselves up with cups of tea. They were discussing the run when the doorbell rang. It had to be Tony Black, late as usual. The guards heard Scouse go down the stairs to let him in. Seconds later, Black walked into the common room. The thirty-one-year-old guard looked pale and drawn as he glanced around the room. He muttered that he needed to go to the toilet, and then went back downstairs.

A couple of minutes later, the guards heard footsteps returning. They paid no attention until a voice bellowed out, 'Get on the floor or you're fucking dead!'

A figure appeared in the doorway of the common room. He was about 5ft 8ins, dressed in a black blazer and black trousers. His face was covered with a canary-yellow balaclava and he brandished a 9mm Browning automatic.

The guards, immobilized by fear, failed to react quickly enough for the intruder's satisfaction. Without a word, he pistol-whipped one of them, sending him crashing to the floor. The other guards quickly dropped to the floor.

'Lie still and keep quiet,' the intruder said in a Cockney accent. As he spoke, two other masked men rushed into the room. Soon the gang had handcuffed all four guards. They also taped their legs together and placed cotton bags, secured with drawstrings, over their heads.

In the radio room, Michael Scouse was suffering a similar ordeal. After letting in the late arrival, Tony Black, Scouse had returned to the radio room. Seconds later he had found himself confronted by two masked men brandishing handguns.

'Are you Scouse?' a voice asked. Scouse nodded and a knife sliced through the front of his jeans. Petrol was poured down his front and over his genitals.

'You'd better do as I say, or I'll put a match to the petrol and a bullet through your head. You have two numbers....What are they?'

With a gun pressed under his chin, Scouse was in no mood for heroics. He shouted the numbers: '94-45-57-85'.

That combination opened the vault door. But there were several other lines of defence which needed to be neutralized before the intruders could reach their treasure.

Below: ***John Palmer, a jeweller in Bath, was acquitted at the Old Bailey in 1987 on charges of handling gold from the Brink's-Mat robbery, and was presented with a congratulatory 'All Gold' Easter egg by the press.***

They were fully conversant with the sophisticated arrangement of silent alarms, combinations and time locks. And they knew exactly what authority Scouse had as shift supervisor. There was no way to bluff them, so Scouse had no option but to lead them through the maze of defences.

As the robbers stepped into the vault, their attention was immediately focused on the three safes at the far end of the room. They totally ignored the stacks of small boxes, bound with metal straps, which littered the floor. They didn't know, and Scouse wasn't about to tell them, that these were the real treasure. Each of these inconspicuous little boxes contained a gold ingot. Together they were worth more than £25 million.

Scouse explained to the gang leader that he couldn't open the safes alone. He had the keys, but only Robin Risley knew that day's combination. Risley was dragged down to the vault and was told to enter the relevant numbers.

Risley was in a panic. The safe numbers had just been changed and he had barely committed them to memory. As he fumbled with the dials, the intruders became increasingly impatient. As Risley continued to struggle with the locks and pleaded with the Cockney, another member of the gang asked Scouse what was in the boxes. Scouse, realizing that it was the only chance to save Risley and probably himself, told him that they contained bullion.

The man ripped open one of the boxes and saw that Scouse was telling the truth. Immediately the gang lost interest in Risley and the safes, and turned their attention to shifting the three tons of gold into the loading bay.

The gang leader asked Scouse how the shutter doors to the loading bay opened. Scouse replied that that was Tony Black's job. The leader went back upstairs. 'Which one of you is Black?' he asked. Black, who was lying in a pool of petrol on the office floor, identified himself and was frog-marched into the radio room at knifepoint. He opened the shutter doors by remote control, and a van drove into the warehouse.

Fifteen minutes later the same van drove out again, suspension groaning under the weight of £26 million worth of gold, the biggest haul in criminal history.

Within minutes of Michael Scouse freeing himself and raising the alarm, the Flying Squad were at the scene of the robbery. The investigation was headed by Commander Frank Cater.

From the outset, Cater had no doubt that this was an inside job. The most obvious suspects were the guards. They had all been taken to the casualty department of Ashford Hospital. The pistol-whipped Peter Bentley was treated for head wounds, and Scouse and Risley were suffering from petrol burns. The other men were unhurt.

By 10a.m., all six men were being grilled by Cater and his team at Hounslow police station.

PRIME SUSPECT

The most obvious suspects, because of their special knowledge and responsibilities, were Scouse and Risley. But, as the morning wore on and more information about the six men came into the incident room, another name caught Cater's eye.

Anthony John Black stuck out like a sore thumb. He did not have a criminal record himself, but his common-law brother-in-law, Brian Robinson, was well known to the police.

Despite the fact that he was sure that Black was the man he was after, Commander Cater elected to send him home along with the other guards. At 8 a.m. on Sunday, 4 December, more than a week after the raid, detectives arrived simultaneously at the homes of all six guards and invited them down to Hounslow police station for further questioning. Five of the guards were asked to go over their statements again. It was all routine.

Tony Black, however, was given the full treatment. His interrogation, led by Detective Inspector Tony Brightwell, lasted more than six hours as they went over his statement again and again in minute detail.

Then Detective Sergeant Alan Branch dropped his bombshell. He looked Black straight in the eye and asked, 'What does your brother-in-law think about the robbery?'

BLACK WAS ALLOWED HOME, NOT REALIZING THAT THE POLICE WERE CONVINCED HE HAD BEEN IN ON THE ROBBERY

THE SECURITY GUARD HAD PROVIDED THE ROBBERS WITH PHOTOGRAPHS, KEYS AND DETAILED INFORMATION

The fact that the police knew about his connection with Brian Robinson obviously shook Black, but he was not ready to fold yet. The game of cat and mouse lasted until 3p.m. the following day. The police piled more and more pressure on the prisoner and he was obviously getting ready to crack.

'Can I have a cup of tea?' Black asked.

Detective Sergeant Nicholas Benwell left the interview room and returned with a plastic cup from the vending machine. Black took a sip and looked up.

'Where do I start?' he asked.

MOLE TURNS GRASS

When Tony Black decided to talk, he talked with a vengeance. It took Sergeant Benwell more than eight hours to take down his statement. He explained how he had been approached by his sister's common-law husband, Brian Robinson, to provide inside information about shipments, security arrangements, the layout of the warehouse and details of personnel and procedures. Black admitted that on the day of the robbery, he had let the gang into the warehouse.

According to Black, Robinson had two

Below: ***John Palmer's house outside Bath. Armed police raided the house on the morning after the death of DC Fordham, but found Palmer and his wife had left for a holiday in the Canary Islands.***

accomplices. One was a man in his early thirties called Mick. The other was a giant of a man who went by the name of Tony.

Shortly after Black finished his statement, Detective Sergeant Branch came into the interview room with two files containing mugshots of known associates of Brian Robinson. Black leafed through the photographs and did not hesitate in identifying two of them – Tony White and Mick McAvoy.

Having broken every rule in the criminal code book, Tony Black was taken back to his cell.

At 6.30 the following morning, Tuesday 6 December, the Flying Squad picked up Robinson, McAvoy and White. The three men were taken to separate police stations well away from Hounslow. Robinson was polite but firm in his denial of any wrongdoing, and provided the police with a detailed alibi for the day of the robbery. White was aggressive and blunt. McAvoy would say nothing without his lawyer being present.

Under normal circumstances, Frank Cater knew that breaking the three men down would take time. He decided to take a short cut. He showed them Tony Black's statement. White was the first to capitulate. He admitted being a party to the robbery and wanted to explore the possibility of doing a deal. At the end of the interview, however, White refused to sign his statement and he would later withdraw his admission of guilt at his trial.

Brian Robinson realized that, in the light of Black's testimony, his position was hopeless. He admitted that he had helped set up the robbery but denied being involved in the execution of the crime itself.

McAvoy stuck to his tactic of silence until he too had read Black's statement, at which point he folded completely.

There would be no deal for McAvoy or White, but there certainly was for Tony Black. On 17 February 1984, Black – the 'Golden Mole' – stood trial at the Old Bailey. In less than an hour he was arraigned, tried and sentenced to six years' imprisonment. This meant that, with full remission and parole, he would serve no more than two years.

Black's next appearance in court was at the Old Bailey in October 1984 – not as the accused but as the chief prosecution witness in the trials of Brian Robinson, Mick McAvoy and Tony White. Black's testimony lasted almost three days and was frequently interrupted by catcalls and abuse from the public gallery. Nobody, it seems, likes a grass.

Since identity parades and forensic evidence had proved inconclusive, the prosecution's case rested almost totally

Above: ***The makeshift smelting shack found in the grounds of John Palmer's house. Inside*** **(below),** ***police discovered a foundry crucible and lifting gear, and in the house itself they came across two ingots of gold, still warm.***

on Black's evidence. In the cases of Brian Robinson and Mick McAvoy, this proved sufficient to convince the jury of their guilt. But Tony White, who claimed the police had tricked and coerced him into his confession, was found not guilty.

The Judge warned Robinson and McAvoy that he had no choice but to impose a heavy sentence of twenty-five years' imprisonment.

ONGOING INVESTIGATION

For the police, the matter did not end with the conviction of Black, Robinson and McAvoy. There was still the small matter of £26 million in gold bullion to be accounted for.

The police used their vast network of criminal intelligence to narrow down the field in their hunt for the Brink's-Mat haul. They came up with a list of names, known associates of Robinson and White. This list included Kenneth Noye, a Kent businessman and property dealer with a considerable criminal pedigree.

After months of investigation, Cater became convinced that Noye was the main link in an elaborate chain through which the Brink's-Mat bullion was being channelled. It went from Noye to his friend Brian Reader and on to Garth Chappell, John Palmer and Scadlynn Ltd, a bullion dealer in Bristol.

The police's main problem was that if they moved in on any member of that chain, the others would be alerted and go to ground. In the short term it was decided to keep the key players under surveillance. Detective Chief Superintendent Brian Boyce, who had taken over the Brink's-Mat case, was sure that at least part of the bullion was being stored at Hollywood Cottage, Noye's Kent mansion.

THE WAITING GAME GOES TRAGICALLY WRONG

By January 1985 Boyce was getting ready to move in. The round-the-clock observation on Hollywood Cottage was intensified. On the evening of Thursday 10 January, Detective Constables John Fordham and Neil Murphy of the elite C11 surveillance unit were sent into the

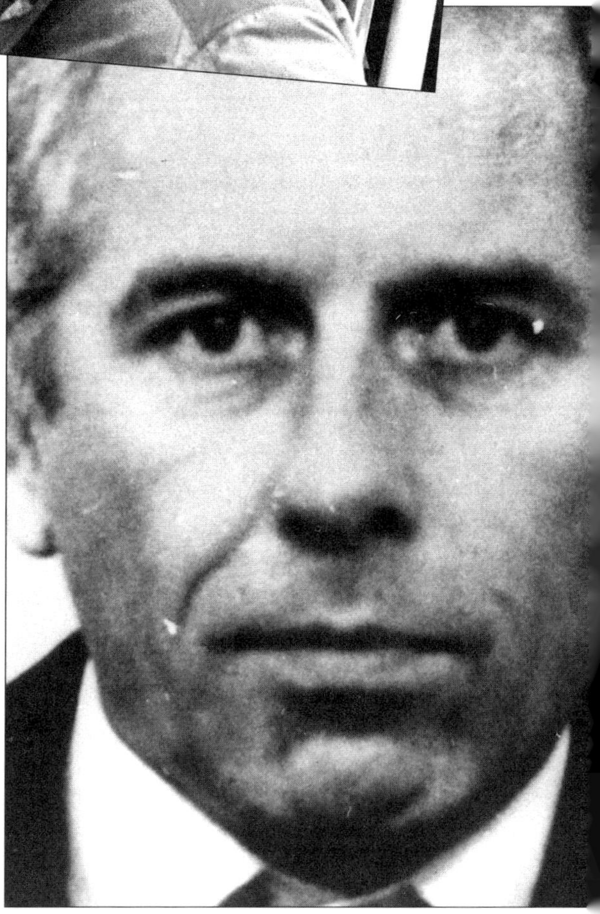

Above and right: ***Scores of suspects were arrested for offences relating to Brink's-Mat. John Fleming (above) was extradited from Miami only to have all charges against him dismissed in less than two minutes by stipendiary magistrate Norma Negus. John Lloyd (right), on the other hand, is still wanted.***

grounds of the house for close observation. Seconds later, three Rottweilers leapt out of the dark.

Murphy made a dash for the perimeter fence. Once safely in the road, he waited for his partner. Detective Constable Fordham never materialized.

Almost half an hour elapsed before Detective Constables David Manning and John Childs went into the grounds of Hollywood Cottage to look for their missing colleague. Almost immediately they saw Fordham lying on his back, with the Rottweilers pulling at his clothes. Standing over the fallen policeman was Kenneth Noye, pointing a shotgun at him.

Manning whipped out his warrant card and shouted, 'I am a police officer.' He walked over to where Fordham was lying and immediately saw blood oozing from his chest and stomach. 'He's done me,' Fordham gasped. 'He's stabbed me.'

Noye was dragged off, and charged with malicious wounding, a charge which had to be changed to murder a few hours later. With the tragic loss of Detective Constable Fordham, the nature of the police operation became public and Boyce had to move quickly.

Within an hour of the stabbing, police raided the home of Brian Reader and discovered almost £70,000 in new £50 notes along with several lumps of yellow-coloured metal. They took these away, together with notebooks, diaries and address books – anything which would help establish Reader's connection with other members of the bullion chain.

The search of Hollywood Cottage and its grounds did provide ample evidence that Kenneth Noye was involved in the Brink's-Mat robbery. In a shallow gully beside the garage wall, they found eleven gold bars, weighing some 13kg and worth something in excess of £100,000.

Nearly fifty officers sealed off the village of Litton, home of Garth Chappell. Inside Chappell's home they discovered a briefcase containing £12,500 in £50 notes. Armed police raided John Palmer's house. Palmer was not there. Three guests at the house informed police that Mr and Mrs Palmer had left the day before with their children for a three-week holiday in the Canary Islands. In the grounds of the house, police found a makeshift smelter. In the house itself they discovered two gold ingots, still warm, along with a selection of firearms, and a large quantity of cash.

It took months for the detectives to piece everything together. As they had suspected, the gold had been passed from Noye to Reader and from him to Chappell. Chappell had paid Reader for each shipment in £50 notes, and Reader had paid Noye.

Once in possession of the gold, Chappell would resmelt it, mixing it with copper to hide its purity. Scadlynn would then sell it on the open market as scrap. In the space of six months, Chappell had managed to dispose of about half of the Brink's-Mat haul – some £13 million worth of gold.

Noye was jailed for thirteen years and fined £250,000. Chappell received ten years and a £200,000 fine. Reader was sentenced to ten years, and John Palmer, who returned from Spain voluntarily, was found not guilty.

Above: ***Gordon Parry was one of many suspects arrested and remanded in custody. In August 1992, he was found guilty and sentenced to ten years' imprisonment.***

ROBERTO SUAREZ
Cocaine Baron

The Bolivian economy is based on a single product – cocaine – and in the 1970s the drug cartel ran their own corrupt and brutal puppet government. Denied US aid as a result, the country faced bankruptcy and its people starved

Narcotics are the boom industry of the post-war era. To organized crime, drugs have always had a very special appeal. They are illegal, addictive and vastly profitable.

In Latin America, the world's leading exporter of cocaine and high-grade marijuana, drug trafficking has grown beyond an illicit activity. It is the backbone of several national economies.

The best-known example of these drug-based economies is Colombia. While accurate figures are impossible to obtain, informed sources estimate that each year Colombia exports something in the region of 100 tons of cocaine with a street value in excess of $60 billion.

The money generated represents approximately 40 per cent of Colombia's gross national product, and by far its biggest source of foreign income. It is understandable, therefore, that government attempts to stamp out the drug industry have been at best half-hearted.

Drug trafficking in Colombia is in the hands of a few powerful and vastly wealthy families. Escabar, Lehder, O'Campo and Ochoa are household names in the drug capitals of Medellin and Cali. These drug traffickers control the police, sponsor politicians, and in reality run the country.

The most powerful of these drug families is Escabar. At forty Pablo Escabar, the head of the family, is a veteran of the drug industry. His wealth is legendary – some estimates place him among the ten richest men in the world.

Based in Medellin where he runs five homes, though technically in hiding from the authorities he is very much a public figure. Escabar has used part of his vast

Left: *A typical cocaine 'laboratory' discovered during one of the operations by Colombian army and police against the Medellin cartel.*

Opposite: *Pablo Escabar, head of the most powerful of Colombian drug families, surrendered to the authorities on 19 June 1991 and was taken to the high-security prison of Envigado.*

Below: *Part of the haul from a drugs raid on a ranch near Buenos Aires, Colombia, in April 1991. More than ten tons of cocaine were found buried.*

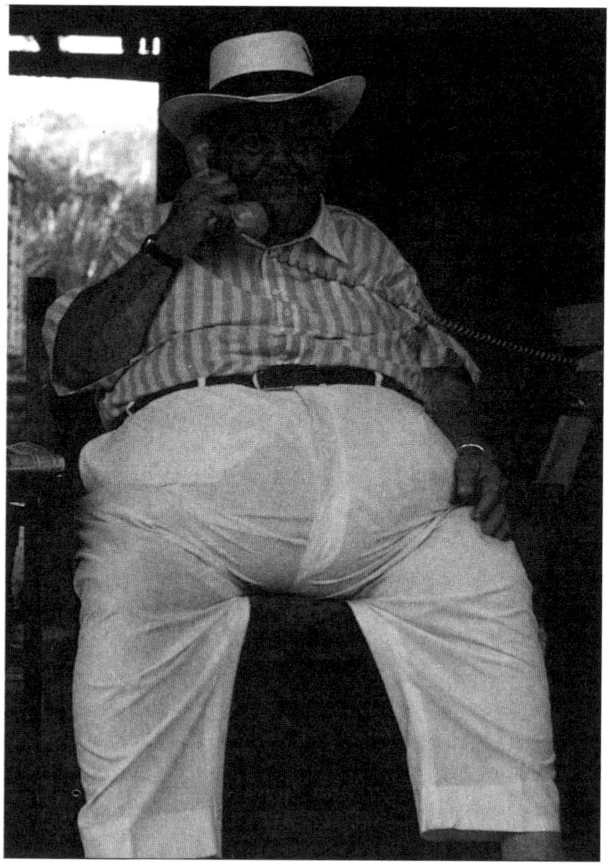

Left: ***Fabio Ochoa, a member of one of Colombia's powerful drug-trafficking families.***

BIGGEST OF THE COLOMBIAN DRUG BARONS, PABLO ESCABAR MAY WELL BE ONE OF THE TEN RICHEST MEN IN THE WORLD

fortune on a rehousing project: he has built thousands of homes for the poor and has thus achieved heroic status in the *barrios* – the slums. That generosity is not entirely altruistic, however. His 'people' feel an intense gratitude towards him and afford him all the protection they can, both from the authorities and from professional rivals.

The other Colombian drug barons, noting Escabar's public acclaim, have followed his example. They have built roads, hospitals and sports facilities, none of which the impoverished Colombian government could possibly afford.

For all this generosity, the drug families are ruthless beyond imagination. The threat of assassination is a reality for any politician who has the gall to speak out against them. Bolivian Justice Minister Rodrigo Lara Bonilla found that out to his cost in 1984, when he died in a hail of bullets while parking his car in Bogota.

The drug families also maintain a ruthless internal discipline. The murder rate in Medellin – a city of just over one million – is more than six a day, most of which are drug-related.

While the American Mafia will execute anyone who breaks their code of Omerta, the Colombian cartels will massacre the culprit's entire family in front of him. Most of the bodies found after such a massacre have been dismembered or tortured. Despite all this, the families' heroic myth persists.

ALL POWER TO THE DRUG BARONS

While Colombia rightly holds the reputation of being the world's leading cocaine exporter, in fact it grows a comparatively small amount of coca leaf – less than 10 per cent of the Latin American crop. Colombia assumed its position of world dominance because of its expertise in refining and distribution.

Most of its raw material comes from Peru or neighbouring Bolivia. And it is Bolivia that boasts the best example of the powers of organized crime. The leading Bolivian drug baron, Roberto Suarez, actually succeeded in installing a government of his choice because he disliked the one that had been elected democratically. The government eventually fell, but Suarez and his organization are still in business.

Roberto Suarez is not typical of the Latin American drug tsars, most of whom clawed their way from the gutter to the

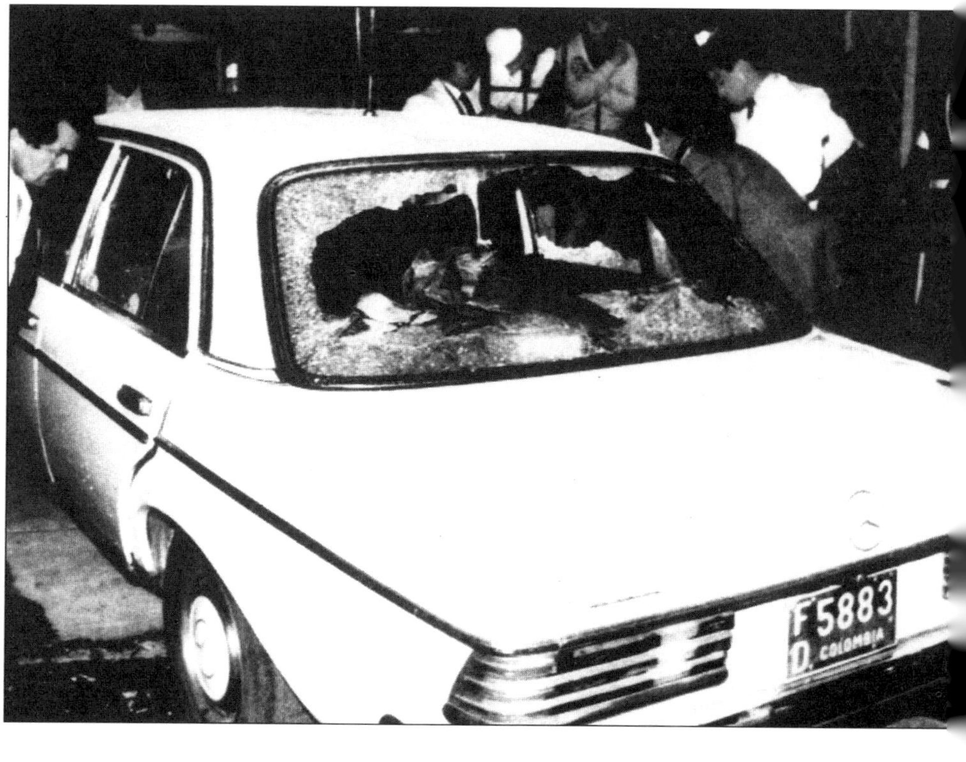

Below: ***The car of Bolivian Justice Minister Rodrigo Lara Bonilla, who was assassinated by gunmen hired by drug barons. The gunmen themselves were subsequently shot by the Minister's bodyguard.***

top of their profession via the ranks of other drug organizations. Suarez is a well-educated man from a rich family.

He started out as a cattle rancher, but soon found that his vast land holdings could be put to more profitable use. Today his coca plantations, scattered around the Beni, Chapare and Santa Cruz regions of Bolivia, grow almost half the coca leaf which eventually makes its way to the United States as refined cocaine.

At a conservative estimate, this yields an annual profit to the Suarez family in the region of $1 billion. Very little of his product is sold directly to the American market. Most is shipped as 'base' to Colombia, to traffickers like Pablo Escabar, who refine and market it.

Like his Colombian counterparts, Roberto Suarez has been lavishly generous. He has built and equipped hospitals, paved roads and helped to house the country's poor.

Despite his education, vast wealth and largesse, however, Suarez has always had all the thuggish trappings of other Latin American drug barons. He had his own private army, the 'Fiancés of Death', who were under the direct control of his security adviser, a meek-looking German called Klaus Altmann.

Altmann was really Klaus Barbie, the ex-Gestapo chief and mass murderer

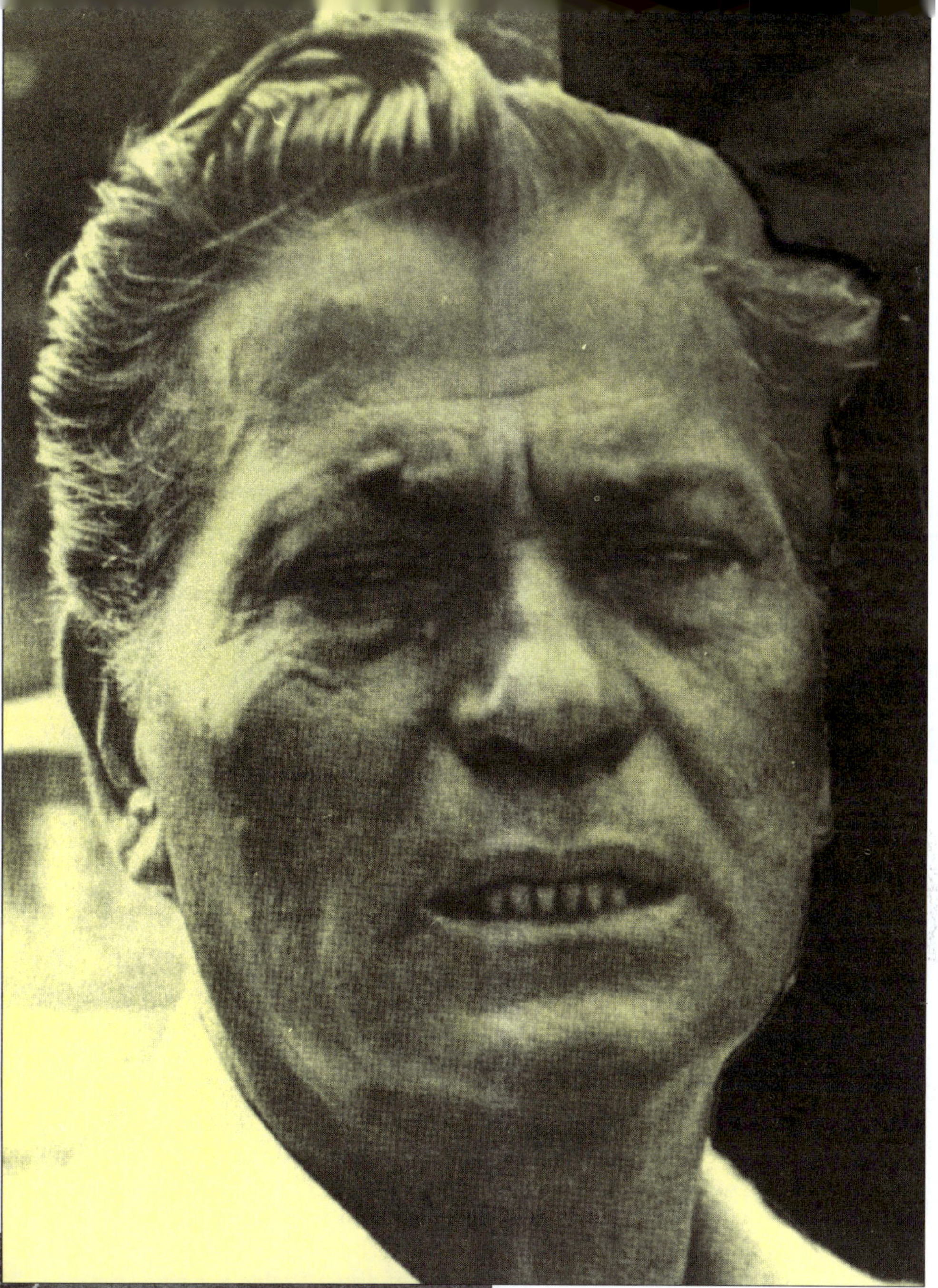

Above: ***Roberto Suarez, the leading Bolivian drug baron, began as a cattle rancher, but soon decided that his vast land holdings could be better put to the growing of coca plants. He is said to produce more than half the coca leaf grown in Bolivia and Colombia.***

Left: ***Suarez's San Vicente ranch, near the city of Santa Ana de Yacuma, Bolivia, could be approached only by air.***

known as the 'Butcher of Lyon', who had escaped from Europe to Bolivia in 1951. Barbie and his army played a key role in Suarez's plans to change the government of Bolivia.

For many years, the cocaine barons of Bolivia had things their own way. From 1971 to 1978 the country was governed by President Hugo Banzer, a trafficker in his own right, who flew wide-bodied transport planes to Colombia from his own private airstrip on an estate in San Javier. But when Banzer was finally deposed and Silus Zuazo was democratically elected, an anti-drug campaign was initiated.

The move was largely ineffective, but Suarez didn't like the way things were going. He called a meeting of drug barons at the Club Bavaria in Santa Cruz to discuss the possibility of change.

ENGINEERED MILITARY COUP

Acting on information from his cousin, Colonel Luis Arce Gomez, Suarez told the assembled company that he believed the Bolivian military might well be prepared to instigate a well-financed coup. Gomez had advised Suarez that the man to approach was General Luis Garcia Meza, the overall army commander. Gomez was paid $800,000 to effect an introduction. He was also given a promise that he would be appointed Minister of the Interior if the coup was successful.

Suarez met with Meza and offered him $1.3 million to lead the coup, making it clear that this was only a nominal down payment on the vast fortune he could expect to accrue if he pulled it off.

On 17 July 1980, General Meza led the 189th coup in the country's 150-year history as an independent state.

As well as Meza's Special Security Service and suppression squads, Klaus Barbie's Fiancés of Death were seconded to Gomez and the Ministry of the Interior. More than five hundred civilians were murdered during the first two weeks of the takeover, and another two and a half thousand were imprisoned and tortured.

Once they had quashed political and civil unrest, the security squads and the Fiancés of Death turned their attention to the smaller cocaine growers and dealers. They smashed their operations, seized their stocks and channelled them through Roberto Suarez and his organization.

These were halcyon days for the favoured traffickers. A Washington expert described the situation grimly: 'It is impossible to calculate the money they made. Think of a preposterous figure, double it and know damned well that you've made a gross underestimate.'

Above: ***At dawn on 21 July 1988 Roberto Suarez was arrested in his hacienda near the Brazilian border by the 'Leopards', a special commando squad put together by Bolivian anti-narcotics forces.***

Right: ***For many years Suarez maintained a private army, the 'Fiancés of Death'. They were controlled by ex-Gestapo chief Klaus Barbie, the 'Butcher of Lyon', who was arrested in 1983 and extradited to France.***

SUAREZ'S PRIVATE ARMY WAS RUN BY A GERMAN CALLED KLAUS ALTMANN. THE WORLD KNOWS HIM BETTER AS KLAUS BARBIE

Meza's government was not only brutal; it was massively inefficient. The effect on the ordinary people of Bolivia was devastating.

Obsessed with cocaine profits, Meza abandoned the stabilization programme which had been introduced by the International Monetary Fund to prop up the country's crumbling economy. He also appeared totally indifferent when, in reaction to the new regime, Washington suspended US aid to Bolivia which should have totalled almost $130 million.

Bolivian industry went totally neglected. Financial chaos reigned and black marketeers sold pesos on street corners.

COSMETIC CLEAN-UP

It was Suarez rather than his puppet government who finally realized that something had to be done to halt the growing ostracization of Bolivia, not just by Washington, but also by its Latin American neighbours. He instructed Meza, himself now a trafficker, to mount a cosmetic operation against narcotics.

Suarez and his friends, of course, were never touched. Only a few independent growers and dealers were purged and their stocks seized.

The whole operation was a farce, but it had the desired effect. In Washington Ronald Reagan praised the apparent change of heart of Meza's government, and there was talk about restoring Bolivia's foreign aid.

The confiscations left Arce Gomez and his ministry with a vast stockpile of coca, which Suarez expected to be handed over for sale to Colombia.

Gomez had ideas above his station, however, and demanded a payment of $50 million. Suarez paid up, but he was enraged by this display of arrogance and ingratitude from his own cousin.

Within weeks he exacted his revenge. He engineered Gomez's dismissal from his post as Minister of the Interior and assumed control of Klaus Barbie and his Fiancés of Death.

Arce Gomez's replacement, General Celso Torrelio Villa, was hand-picked by Suarez, who by now was paymaster to the armed forces. Air force general Waldo Bernal, for instance, was paid $150,000 per week for allowing his planes to be used for shipping coca paste to Colombia.

By late summer, Suarez was becoming disenchanted with Meza and decided he would have to go. The military government, who were all on his payroll, supported him. In September 1981 Meza was overthrown in a military coup and replaced by General Torrelio Villa.

The whole thing was a piece of theatre designed to impress Washington, and it succeeded. President Reagan appointed Edwin Corr, a narcotics expert, as the new US ambassador to La Paz. Corr was taken in and sent positive feedback to his bosses in Washington.

Reagan, however, was still not convinced. In an attempt to persuade the US President, Suarez ordered Torrelio Villa to agree to the extradition of Alfredo Gutierrez and Marcelo Ibanez to Miami, where they were wanted for

Top: ***In 1982 General Guido Vildoso restored power to the exiled Bolivian president Hernan Siles Zuozo, who pledged himself to fight the drug barons.***

Above: ***Suarez's cousin, former Minister of the Interior and drug trafficker Luis Arce Gomez, was finally arrested at his ranch in December 1989.***

trafficking offences. It is a measure of Suarez's determination that both men were old friends and colleagues, and that he himself stood indicted in the same case.

Suarez, however, considered that their deportation was an acceptable sacrifice for the greater good of Bolivia. Ibanez and Gutierrez had ample reason to disagree, as they were jailed for twelve and five years respectively.

In a desperate effort to improve Bolivia's image further, Suarez and his family replaced President Torrelio Villa with General Guido Calderon, who came to office primed to promise democratic elections within the year.

TO RELEASE HIS SON SUAREZ OFFERED TO PAY OFF THE £4 BILLION BOLIVIAN FOREIGN DEBT – A SUM HE DESCRIBED AS 'PETTY CASH'

SHORT-TERM SETBACK

Despite, or maybe because of the changes in government, Roberto Suarez and his organization continued to prosper. In December 1981, however, he suffered a severe setback. His son, Roberto Jnr, was arrested by Swiss immigration authorities while trying to enter Locarno from Madrid on a forged Colombian passport. He was carrying $250,000 in cash and, according to investigators, was waiting for $10 million to be wired from La Paz which he intended to deposit in one of his father's numerous Swiss bank accounts.

The simple passport offence was just what the American authorities had been waiting for. For some time, they had been trying to extradite Suarez Jnr from Bolivia to stand trial along with Gutierrez and Ibanez. The Swiss authorities handed him over to the Americans and he was summarily shipped back to Miami.

Roberto Suarez Snr was prepared to go to any lengths to secure the safe return of his son and heir. He even offered to pay off the entire Bolivian foreign debt which stood at somewhere over $4 billion. The American authorities, of course, were not dealing. Suarez had to content himself with retaining a team of high-priced lawyers to mount his son's defence.

In spite of his personal problems, business for Suarez and his friends had never been better. American DEA intelligence gathered during the year of Calderon's government calculated that in the Chapare and Yungas regions, some 90,000 tons of coca leaf were grown. Five years earlier the same region had produced less than 5000 tons.

Below: ***When Hugo Banzer, a drug trafficker in his own right, became president of Bolivia in 1971, students protested on a large scale. Soldiers with tanks were brought in to control them; hundreds of students were taken prisoner, four killed and 14 injured.***

DEMOCRACY RETURNS

The obscene profits were being harvested by the drug barons, but Bolivia was suffering the worst poverty in Latin America. Industry had now ground to a virtual halt, while unemployment and inflation soared. The peasant class were starving and, with nothing to lose, took to the streets in protest. They demanded the removal of the inept, corrupt military government and the restoration of civilian authority.

Calderon was forced to surrender his office to a civilian administration. Before he did so, however, he allowed Suarez and Meza to ransack the Bolivian Narcotics Board offices and remove all records of their trafficking activities.

In 1982, Hernan Silas Zuozo returned from exile in Peru and started the process of restoring his country to democratic rule. He returned to the office of president with a massive mandate from the people together with support from Washington and other Latin American administrations. In an address to the United Nations, Zuozo expressed gratitude for this support and pledged himself and his administration to fight the drug barons who had brought his country to the brink of extinction.

Zuozo set about living up to his promises. He deported Klaus Barbie to France, where he was tried and convicted of war crimes. Gomez and Meza fled to Argentina rather than face the charges that were levelled against them. There was a purge of the army, and over two hundred officers faced charges in front of courts martial. It was an impressive start, but it was only tokenism. The true fabric of the country remained unchanged, and Suarez continued to run his cocaine empire openly.

Zuozo needed outside help if he was to win his unequal fight against the drug barons, so he turned to the Americans. In April 1983 President Reagan's Attorney General, William French Smith, and Francis Mullen, head of the Drug Enforcement Agency, travelled to La Paz for a meeting with the Bolivian President.

The Americans offered to finance a $40 million crop substitution programme, by which farmers would be offered subsidies to switch from coca production to other less noxious crops. Zuozo signed the appropriate papers and agreed to implement the programme. However, Zuozo simply did not have the power to carry it off. Peasant farmers already living below the poverty line had no intention of abandoning coca for a less profitable crop. Nor did Zuozo have the backing of the army, many of whom were still involved in the drug trade.

Above: ***Roberto Suarez Jr, whose homecoming from remand in Miami was celebrated by a week-long feast. In 1990 he died in a shoot-out with police in the Bolivian city of Santa Cruz.***

SPITTING IN THE WIND

Within weeks of French Smith's visit to Bolivia, the country was to witness ample evidence of the Suarez family's invulnerability. In Miami, after he had spent a year on remand, Roberto Suarez Jnr's legal team successfully argued that much of the DEA's evidence against their client was inadmissible. Without this evidence, the prosecution case collapsed and young Suarez was found not guilty.

Santa de Yacuma had never seen a fiesta to compare with the one thrown to celebrate Roberto Jnr's homecoming. Bands greeted his aircraft and five thousand townsfolk celebrated day and night all week, spurred on by a limitless supply of whiskey and wine flown in from the capital, La Paz. The celebrations were dominated by Roberto Suarez Snr. He arrived at the airport in one of his own highly recognizable fleet of aircraft. The blatant arrogance of the gesture was not lost on American observers.

Below: ***The estate of Colombian drug baron Rodriguez Gacha, which was seized by the authorities in August 1989.***

KHUN SA
Opium Warlord

In a mountain fastness on the borders with Thailand, Burma and Laos dwells one of the most powerful businessmen on earth. Khun Sa is Asia's opium warlord, immune to the might of governments and drug enforcement agencies all over the world

The Golden Triangle is the world's most prolific poppy garden. Bounded by the Mekong and Mae Si rivers where Thailand, Burma and Laos meet, the Triangle consists of 80,000 square miles of mountainous jungle terrain. With no roads and few paths, it is virtually unpoliced and unpoliceable.

Only the mountain people, the Shan, can negotiate the area with any safety, and the Shan owe their allegiance to none of the three countries which have technical sovereignty over their

Left: ***Two of Khun Sa's 5,000-strong, heavily armed private army that patrols the borders of his 'kingdom'.***

Opposite: ***Khun Sa ruler of the Golden Triangle.***

Below: ***In 1982 the Thai army mounted a massive attack on Khun Sa's new headquarters at Ban Hin Taek to impress the US Attorney General William French Smith.***

homeland. They know only one authority, Khun Sa, a feudal warlord and the most powerful heroin dealer in the world.

AN EMPIRE BUILT ON POPPIES

Khun Sa's rule over the Golden Triangle, and thereby his control of its drug trade, is absolute. His status is maintained with the help of a 5,000-strong private army.

From his fortress villas, Khun Sa runs a drug empire which produces more than sixty tons of heroin a year. Local demand for opium and heroin is huge, but even when this has been satisfied he has a twenty-ton surplus for export.

But Khun Sa is a shrewd marketing man, and he rations these exports carefully. He never floods the market, which would depress the price. And he always maintains a stockpile as insurance against a poor poppy harvest.

MILITARY ORIGINS

Khun Sa is about sixty years old, the son of a Chinese father and a Shan mother. His father was a colonel in Chiang Kai-shek's Chinese Nationalist 'Kuomintang' army which fled south into Burma after their defeat by the Communists in 1949.

Long after this defeat, the Kuomintang army remained intact as a functioning fighting force in the Shan province of northern Burma. They were welcomed by the Shan tribesmen, who were themselves in conflict with their central government in Rangoon. The Kuomintang army recruited Shan peasants into its ranks and re-named themselves the 'Anti-Communist Army of National Safety'.

Chiang Kai-shek, who was safely ensconced in Taiwan, saw this exiled force as his second front for a planned reconquest of China.

The Americans, who had supported Chiang, also welcomed their presence in northern Burma. They saw this force as a safeguard against the spread of Communism, and for more than a decade supplied them with money, arms and equipment.

Even the Burmese government tolerated their presence, because they too were worried about the Communist Chinese on their northern border.

In the late 1950s, however, the Burmese thought the Kuomintang were getting too powerful and drove them across the border into Thailand and Laos.

In 1961, the Americans also became disenchanted with this forgotten army and all official aid was stopped. While

Right: ***Khun Sa addressing recruits to his private army at Tiger Camp across the Burmese border.***

THE SHAN TRIBESMEN ARE SPREAD OVER THREE COUNTRIES, BUT THEIR ONLY TRUE ALLEGIANCE IS TO KHUN SA

EVEN AFTER SATISFYING THE HUGE LOCAL DEMAND, THERE IS STILL AN ANNUAL TWENTY-TON SURPLUS OF OPIUM AND HEROIN FOR EXPORT

Below: ***A Karen tribes-woman inspects the developing crop of opium poppies near Chiang Mai in Thailand.***

only cash crop which would grow in the inhospitable mountains of the Golden Triangle. While opium had been made illegal by the Burmese government in the early 1950s, the administration had turned a blind eye to the illicit harvest in the north.

In the 1960s the Shan accepted the Kuomintang leaders' suggestion that they take over the refining and marketing of their crop.

they continued to receive covert aid and support from the CIA for another fifteen years, the Kuomintang's income had been drastically cut.

It was at this time that the army leaders moved into the opium trade in a big way.

The Shan peasants had been cultivating poppies for centuries as the

AFTER US AID STOPPED, THE KUOMINTANG FINANCED THEMSELVES BY TAKING OVER THE SHANS' COTTAGE INDUSTRY OF POPPY CULTIVATION

Left: ***The crop is ripe at Mong Mao in Burma. The raw opium oozes from slits made in the poppy-seed bulbs and is scraped off.***

OFFICIAL US POLICY OUTLAWED HEROIN DEALERS LIKE KHUN SA, BUT THE CIA USED HIM AS AN INTELLIGENCE SOURCE

BACKED BY THE CIA

It was in this confusing environment that the young Khun Sa grew up. Everything he knew about the opium trade he learned from his father and the Kuomintang commanding officer, General Li Mi.

By the early 1960s, Khun Sa had risen through the command structure of the Kuomintang to become its leader and main contact with the CIA. For years he supplied the CIA headquarters in Langley, Virginia with information about Communist activity in the region, and at the same time was exporting heroin to America on a massive scale.

In the mid-1960s and 1970s, under the administrations of Johnson, Nixon and Carter, a truly absurd situation developed. Washington had declared all-out war on heroin dealers like Khun Sa, yet the CIA was busy keeping him in business as an intelligence source.

The situation became even more complicated, and Khun Sa's loyalties were stretched even thinner, when the Americans went into Vietnam.

Drug abuse, and particularly heroin abuse, among American servicemen was epidemic. Figures suggest that as many as one in seven were drug-dependent, and certainly towards the end of the war more soldiers were evacuated for drug rehabilitation than for combat injuries.

The Vietcong certainly capitalized on the situation and so did Khun Sa. Despite his avowed anti-Communist standpoint and his close relationship with the CIA, he smuggled vast quantities of heroin into South Vietnam.

American soldiers represented a rich and readily accessible market to him, and he was indifferent to their political and military aims. They were customers.

Above: *In 1987 Khun Sa, after two decades as the unchallenged ruler of the Golden Triangle, held a press conference at his Burmese headquarters.*

TRIAD INVOLVEMENT

Thus the late 1960s and early 1970s were a boom period for Khun Sa. To cater for the ever-growing demand for heroin, he encouraged Thai farmers to increase their output and established a string of new refineries along the Burmese-Thai border.

Like all his laboratories, these were in inaccessible mountain locations. The refined heroin was transported under armed guard to Bangkok, by mule train or elephant.

The middle-men in Bangkok, who handled the distribution for Khun Sa, were for the most part Chinese. They were members of various Triad Societies and came from Hong Kong, Malaysia and Singapore. Most of the original Kuomintang Army – including General Li and Chiang Kai-shek himself – had been members of the Triads, and so Khun Sa understood them and their codes of conduct.

But while he was happy to deal with them in their capacity as wholesalers, he resisted any attempt by the Triads to become involved in the growing or refining of opium in his domain. When Limpy Ho, Godfather of Hong Kong, came personally to the Golden Triangle to discuss the purchase of raw opium for processing in his new Kowloon refinery, he was sent away with a flea in his ear.

Below: *Khun Sa appealed for American help in fighting Communist forces that threatened his power.*

CORRUPTION AND DOUBLE-CROSS

Khun Sa's organization is extremely efficient and has always run with the active support of the notoriously corrupt Thai police. When an independent laboratory was raided by the Thai drug enforcement agency in 1974, it was found to be managed by the deputy divisional commander of police, Lieutenant Colonel Sawai Pudharek.

During his trial, Pudharek escaped through a lavatory window when his police guards' backs were turned. He took off to the mountains and was last heard of managing a laboratory for Khun Sa in Burma.

One of the stipulations placed on the Chinese chemists who ran Khun Sa's laboratories was that they should produce a quality product which would satisfy his customers. American servicemen disliked the coarse brown smoking heroin – No.3 – which was produced for local consumption. They wanted the finer, white powder – No.4 – which was suitable for intravenous injection.

In 1975, when the Americans pulled out of Vietnam, one might have expected Khun Sa's trade to fall off. Not so. His American customers went home addicted and Khun Sa merely arranged for their heroin to be shipped to them.

Not only did he keep the Vietnam veterans supplied, he found a rich new street market in America which more than compensated him for the additional expense and inconvenience of shipping his wares 8000 miles. Besides, the profits were staggering.

Drug Enforcement Agency experts have prepared a financial breakdown on a single kilogram of heroin. In 1975, Khun Sa was paying about $3000 for enough raw opium to produce one kilo of heroin.

Above: *Part of a mule caravan, with heavily armed guerrilla escort, bringing raw opium down from the poppy fields.*

This would sell to a distributor in Bangkok for about $20,000.

By the time this same kilo hit the streets of New York in its nickel bags, it would have changed hands up to six times, each time being cut with lactose or talcum powder, and would retail for upwards of $3 million.

Despite his exploits in Vietnam, Khun Sa was still in communication with the CIA, to whom he sent intelligence reports on Communist activity in the region. In 1978, he contacted them with a proposal for President Carter.

The sheer cheek of it was astonishing. He offered them a solution to the growing American heroin problem. He suggested that, for a consideration of $30 million, he could supply 500 tons of opium direct to the American government over the next five years, thus taking it off the market.

Washington was seriously considering the proposal, but DEA officials talked the government out of it. Their intelligence suggested that Khun Sa could fulfil this obligation and still have enough left over to supply his current illicit markets.

In 1980, armed with his vast fortune, Khun Sa built himself a new, even grander villa at Ban Hin Taek, a small Thai mountain village just five miles on horseback from the Burmese border. He chose the location to provide a quick escape route should he be attacked.

AFTER THE VIETNAM WAR MANY OF KHUN SA'S CUSTOMERS WENT HOME TO AMERICA – SO HE STARTED SHIPPING THEIR NEEDS TO THEM

THE STREET PRICE OF HEROIN IN THE USA IS ABOUT A THOUSAND TIMES THE COST OF RAW OPIUM IN THE GOLDEN TRIANGLE

The Thai government did occasionally launch forays against his laboratories. These were generally fairly half-hearted affairs which served mainly as a PR operation for the benefit of the American Drug Enforcement Agency, who contributed some $6 million a year to Thailand's fight against narcotics.

DEATH IN THE GOLDEN TRIANGLE

By 1980, the DEA had finally woken up to the fact that Khun Sa was not a champion in their fight against Communism and put a bounty of $25,000 on his head. In response, Khun Sa offered a cash reward for any American killed in the Triangle. A few weeks later, the wife of DEA agent Michael Powers was shot dead in the main street of Chiang Mai.

In 1982, when the US Attorney General, William French Smith, was in Bangkok, the Thais did actually mount a serious attack against Khun Sa's new headquarters at Ban Hin Taek. They sent in more than two thousand police and troops, supported by bombers and helicopter gunships.

A bloody battle ensued, during which more than two hundred of Khun Sa's troops were killed. The authorities captured more than ten tons of weapons – seven hundred rifles, grenade launchers,

Above: ***In Chiang Mai, a regular destination on the tourist trail in Thailand, traders cheerfully sell T-shirts advertising opium and the Golden Triangle.***

grenades, bazookas and fifty thousand rounds of ammunition – together with refining equipment and millions of dollars' worth of heroin.

While the raid was in progress, Khun Sa slipped across the border into Burma with most of his army. He set up home in a village called Mong Young in the heart of the Communist-controlled region of the country.

The Communists were poppy growers on a huge scale and used the proceeds to finance their army. Khun Sa immediately did a deal with them, by which he obtained exclusive rights to distribute their surplus heroin overseas.

This arrangement came to the notice of the Burmese authorities in Rangoon, who had thus far tolerated Khun Sa in the mistaken belief that he was actively fighting Communism in their northern territories. Now he was very definitely *persona non grata*.

KHUN SA'S REVENGE ON HIS BETRAYERS WAS TERRIBLE – ONE WAS BURNT ALIVE, ANOTHER PUBLICLY HANGED, DRAWN AND QUARTERED

The Burmese government launched periodic raids against his refineries on the Burmese-Thai border. But, despite being suitably equipped by the Americans, they ducked the challenge of launching an all-out attack against Khun Sa and his army.

In 1984, Khun Sa decided to return to Ban Hin Taek. He had lost a certain amount of face by fleeing Thailand two years earlier and he exacted a terrible revenge on his betrayers. One of the suspected informants was buried alive, another was hanged, drawn and quartered in the main street of the village.

INVULNERABILITY

His position thus consolidated, Khun Sa got back to the real business of refining and selling heroin. Eight years on, and Khun Sa continues to prosper. The combined efforts of the Thai, American and United Nations drug agencies seem powerless to do anything about it.

But it is no longer a question of lack of will. The Thais have a vested interest in curbing the flow of heroin from the Golden Triangle. Drug abuse among their own population has reached epidemic proportions, with more than a million addicts out of a total population of less than 50 million.

The government in Bangkok has taken measures, of course, some of which are considered draconian in the West. They have, for instance, introduced the death penalty for drug trafficking. The trouble is that so far only a handful of small-time Thai street-dealers and the occasional

European tourist have been caught.

The government has also launched raids against opium plantations in the north but, even according to their own figures, they have only succeeded in destroying about 5 per cent of the crop in any given season. They have also banned the import and sale of acetic anhydride, essential in the refining of opium.

Khun Sa got round this problem without difficulty, however. He merely shifted his supply line from the jungle tracks of Thailand to the inland waterways of Burma.

The main problem facing the Thai government is in the very nature of the Golden Triangle itself. It is huge and hostile and would be impossible to police effectively, even with the full cooperation of the local population. And this they certainly do not have.

The Shan tribesmen are vehemently opposed to any attempt to oust Khun Sa, and any clamp-down on the opium trade would be catastrophic for them. More than 25 per cent of them are addicted to opium or heroin, and those who are not rely on poppy growing for survival.

The Shans scoff at crop-substitution programmes. They have always grown poppies, and for a very good reason. Heroin is a high-value, small-volume product which can be transported easily along the winding jungle paths. Try that with kidney beans.

For any such programme to work, the government would have to establish a network of roads through the Triangle, as well as introduce an elaborate irrigation system. The cost would be staggering and, even if they could manage it, any such development would be viewed with deep suspicion by the Shan.

They have lived in splendid isolation for centuries – they don't even speak Thai – and any move to integrate them into mainstream Thailand would be seen as an attempt to take away their independence and destroy their culture.

For more than forty years, they have seen Khun Sa and his predecessors from the Kuomintang army as the only form of central control and stability in Shan province. Khun Sa himself is seen as their protector and provider, and any attempt to remove him would be deemed an attempt to usurp a legitimate power.

Thus protected by both his people and his army, Khun Sa appears invulnerable, and the flow of heroin from the Golden Triangle is destined to continue unstemmed.

Above: ***The Thai assault on Ban Hin Taek failed in its intention to capture Khun Sa, who fled over the border into Burma. The stronghold was destroyed, but Khun Sa returned two years later.***

WHEN THE THAIS BANNED THE IMPORT OF A CHEMICAL ESSENTIAL IN OPIUM REFINING, KHUN SA BROUGHT IT IN THROUGH BURMA

Left: ***The Thai government has introduced the death penalty for drug trafficking, and regularly destroys the quantities of drugs that are seized.***

A CITY SCANDAL
The Guinness Affair

The Guinness share scandal was the biggest fraud the City of London had seen for decades. 'When men are hell-bent on victory, greed is in the saddle,' said the judge as he handed out prison sentences to some of the top names in finance

Above: ***Financier Sir Jack Lyons received £3 million in fees in return for his part in the share-support scheme.***

For those who get away with it, the rewards of corporate fraud can be staggering – and yet, compared with blue-collar crime, the risks are comparatively small. On the occasions when corporate fraud is prosecuted, the sentences imposed on white-collar criminals are generally a fraction of those deemed fit for their less salubrious counterparts. Why is this so?

More often than not, the fraud is an inside job perpetrated by a trusted employee. The company victimized is often so embarrassed by the situation that it decides to cut its losses and fire the culprit. The second reason is that many corporate frauds are so complex that it takes professionals months to unravel the details. Britain's Crown Prosecution Service reckons there is little chance of a lay jury being able to follow the intricacies of the fraud and thereby reach a suitable verdict. There are, of course, exceptions to this rule.

THE CHANCES OF A JURY BEING ABLE TO FOLLOW THE INS-AND-OUTS OF A COMPLICATED FRAUD CASE ARE VERY SLIGHT

THE ACCUSED WOULD HAVE SEEMED MORE AT HOME IN A PALL MALL CLUB THAN IN THE DOCK AT SOUTHWARK CROWN COURT

THE MESS WHICH WAS GUINNESS

February 1990 saw the start of the most sensational fraud trial of the century. The accused would have seemed more at home in the Carlton Club, discussing high finance, than in the dock of Southwark Crown Court facing charges under the Theft Act, the Companies Act and the Prevention of Fraud (Investments) Act.

The four businessmen: Ernest

Opposite: ***Ernest Saunders was brought in to sort out the financial problems at Guinness.***

Left: ***Lord Iveagh, head of the brewing side of the Guinness family.***

Saunders, Chief Executive of Guinness; city wheeler-dealer Anthony Parnes; financier Sir Jack Lyons; and mega-rich industrialist Gerald Ronson – stood accused of theft, false accounting and conspiracy to defraud.

In 1976, Saunders had moved to Switzerland and a post as senior marketing manager with Nestlé. He might have finished his career there had he not been head-hunted by Guinness Plc.

In 1981, Guinness was in desperate need of someone to revive its ailing fortunes. Figures released that June showed its profits down by almost 15 per cent. Lord Iveagh, head of the brewing side of the Guinness family, announced that a cut in the dividend to shareholders would be necessary. The markets responded by sending the Guinness share price plummeting to an all-time low of 50p. After protracted negotiations, Saunders joined Guinness as managing director in October 1981 on a salary of £73,000 per annum.

Within a matter of weeks, Saunders had retained the services of an American-based management consultancy, Bain & Co., to help him untangle the mess which was Guinness. Bain's UK representative was Sir Jack Lyons, later to become Saunders's co-defendant.

Above: ***Olivier Roux was financial director at Guinness at the time of the share-support scheme.***

Right: ***Roger Seelig was a member of the team that advised Saunders during the takeover battle for Distillers.***

WHEN SAUNDERS JOINED GUINNESS IT WAS OVER-BURDENED WITH SUBSIDIARIES RANGING FROM FISH FARMING TO BABIES' POTTIES

Lyons introduced Saunders to his associate, Frenchman Olivier Roux. Roux had a sharp financial brain and complemented Saunders's marketing skills perfectly. He soon became Saunders's right-hand man, and was later appointed Guinness's financial director.

When Saunders arrived at Guinness it had hundreds of subsidiaries ranging from fish farming to the manufacture of babies' potties. Many of these were found to be losing money or at best treading water, and over the next few years Saunders and Roux sold or shut down no fewer than 149 of them.

These ruthless tactics worked. By the end of 1982, profits were up by 10 per cent and the financial press were beginning to notice Saunders. The fortunes of Guinness continued to improve, as did Saunders's reputation. By January 1984, Guinness shares had risen

to 120p and the company's overall worth had grown from £90 million to £200 million.

This very success, however, made Guinness vulnerable. The mid-1980s were a time of takeover fever, and middle-sized, highly profitable, high-profile companies like Guinness were just what the sharks were after.

The only form of defence was attack. By the end of 1984 Saunders' had set his sights on the whisky distillers Arthur Bell.

Their bid was hostile – that is to say, the management of Bells did not want to sell. The Guinness campaign was mounted in utmost secrecy, using specially rented offices and code-names to camouflage their tactics. In June 1985, Saunders announced that he had acquired 70 per cent of Bell's shares.

The financial press once again lionized Saunders, whom they now saw to be expanding Guinness, essentially a one-product company, into a broad-based international drinks empire. Saunders went along with that and, within a few days, he set his sights on the ultimate prize – the whisky giant Distillers.

DISTILLERS – A PRIZE TOO HIGH

Distillers were the market leader in Scotch whisky, with thirty brands including Johnnie Walker, Haig and Dewar's, as well as Booth's and Gordon's gin. Saunders was not, however, alone in wanting to acquire Distillers. James Gulliver, head of the Argyll retail chain, was already in the process of trying to acquire Distillers and he had a head start on Guinness.

In the light of this, Saunders assembled a formidable team of experts to advise and back him. They included Roger Seelig, takeover wizard from Morgan Grenfell; American lawyer Tom Ward; David Mayhew from brokers Cazenove; and Anthony Salz from Freshfields – as well as his established team from Bain, headed by Olivier Roux.

Distillers, under their chairman John Connell, did not want to be taken over but were realistic about the situation. If they had to be swallowed up, they much preferred the idea of a merger with Guinness, a prestige drinks company, to a takeover by Argyll.

On Sunday, 19 January 1986, Distillers' board met at their offices in Mayfair and, after a twelve-hour marathon, reached a unanimous decision. They would recommend to the Distillers' shareholders that they accept a Guinness offer worth £2.2 billion. Guinness, of course, didn't have £2.2 billion, and it was up to Ernest Saunders to raise it in a hurry.

He had a meeting with Sir Thomas Risk, chairman of the Bank of Scotland, and persuaded him to accept the post of chairman of a holding board which would oversee Distillers and Guinness after the proposed merger.

Argyll was not about to take the situation lying down. James Gulliver was

Above: ***Anthony Parnes, known in the City as 'The Animal'.***

THE HOSTILE BID FOR BELL'S WAS MOUNTED IN UTMOST SECRECY, WITH ALL THE PARAPHERNALIA OF A SPY OPERATION

Above: ***Saunders with his son and daughter, who supported him throughout his trial.***

Right: ***Ernest Saunders' home.***

DISTILLERS' DIRECTORS RECOMMENDED SHAREHOLDERS TO ACCEPT THE £2 BILLION BID – BUT GUINNESS DID NOT HAVE £2 BILLION

LONRHO'S TINY ROWLAND EAGERLY SNAPPED UP THE FIVE WHISKY BRANDS THAT DISTILLERS SOLD TO CIRCUMVENT THE MONOPOLIES COMMISSION

relying on the Guinness-Distillers merger being turned down, or at least delayed by the Office of Fair Trading and the Monopolies and Mergers Commission.

Saunders, meanwhile, was lobbying furiously. He enlisted the help of Sir Gordon Reece, Margaret Thatcher's public relations adviser, to argue his case with the Commission. It was to no avail. Sir Gordon Borrie of the OFT would not approve the merger and referred it to the Monopolies Commission. It appeared that Guinness was sunk.

Saunders, however, moved quickly. He proposed to the OFT that Distillers sell off five of their whisky brands, thus taking their combined market share below the critical 25 per cent. Tiny Rowland of Lonrho snapped up the surplus brands for a bargain basement price of £3.5 million. At the same time Guinness upped its offer to £2.35 billion. On 21 March 1986, the Office of Fair Trading gave its official blessing to the Guinness bid. The gloves were off for a knock-down drag-out between Ernest Saunders of Guinness and James Gulliver of Argyll.

The fight soon got thoroughly nasty, with accusations on both sides of smear tactics, espionage, buggings and break-ins. But this was nothing compared with what was to come. The line between legality and illegality in takeover battles has always been fine and, in their quest to win Distillers, Saunders and his team sailed clear across that line.

'THE ANIMAL'

In their bid to woo Distillers' shareholders, both Guinness and Argyll were offering either cash or shares in their own companies in exchange for shares in Distillers. Argyll countered Guinness's new offer with a bid of £2.5 billion. Guinness stood at £2.35 billion, but any increase in the value of its shares would increase the value of its offer.

Guinness shares started to shoot up and with them the value of the Guinness offer for Distillers. Someone was ploughing a vast amount of money into Guinness. The question was, who?

Officially, Guinness retained the services of two companies of stockbrokers – Wood Mackenzie and Cazenove. Unofficially, however, Saunders and Roux had an arrangement with one Anthony Parnes.

Known in the City as 'The Animal', Parnes made his money by introducing rich clients to brokers and collecting some of the commission.

Guinness would prove his most lucrative client ever. During the year that he worked on that company's behalf he collected more than £3 million in commission and fees.

Above: ***Industrialist Gerald Ronson and his wife. Ronson was convicted for his part in the share-support scheme.***

Parnes had a great number of contacts in the City, on Wall Street and beyond, and his job for Guinness was to act as a go-between in a secret and illegal scheme to boost the price of its shares. Money men were approached to buy shares in Guinness and given guarantees against financial loss.

Parnes had no shortage of takers for his 'sure thing'. Gerald Ronson, head of the Heron Corporation, the second largest private company in Britain, came in for £25 million. He was later paid £800,000 by Guinness to cover his losses, together with a £5 million fee when Guinness finally won control of Distillers.

IN ONE YEAR PARNES WAS TO POCKET MORE THAN £3 MILLION IN COMMISSION AND FEES FROM A SINGLE CUSTOMER – GUINNESS

Similarly, Lyons's fees from Guinness would eventually amount to £3 million, which was lodged in a Swiss bank in the name of a Panamanian company. He claimed that this payment was for lobbying services, but in fact he too was a part of the share-support scheme.

Soon money was also flooding into the Guinness coffers from overseas. Never far from a fast buck, Ivan Boesky got into the picture. The American takeover parasite spent £100 million buying Guinness shares. A few weeks later, Guinness invested the same sum in a fund started by Boesky.

With all this going on, it is hardly surprising that Guinness shares shot up 25 per cent in the space of four weeks. This gave Saunders the leverage he needed. On Friday, 18 April 1986 he announced that Guinness now owned 50.7 per cent of Distillers' shares.

BROKEN PROMISES

Saunders immediately moved to assume personal control of the newly formed conglomerate, now valued at almost £4 billion. He chose to ignore his promise to potential shareholders and to Sir Thomas Risk that he, Risk, would be chairman of the holding board. Three weeks after the merger was completed, Saunders told Risk that his services were no longer required. Saunders would take the post of chairman himself.

All hell broke loose. The Guinness stockbrokers Wood Mackenzie resigned, and Saunders was called in by the Governor of the Bank of England and the Scottish Secretary, Malcolm Rifkind, both of whom wanted an explanation.

Saunders had to back down. A new board of non-executive directors was assembled under the chairmanship of Sir Norman Macfarlane. It had the power to hire and fire company executives, including Ernest Saunders.

This was a bitter blow. But on the other side of the Atlantic, real trouble was brewing for Saunders and his allies. In November, Ivan Boesky was arrested for 'insider trading' and was offered a deal. If he cooperated with the Securities and Exchange Commission, some of the charges against him would be dropped.

On Wall Street the big question being pondered was: who would Ivan Boesky take down with him?

THE INVESTIGATION

On 1 December 1986 two men arrived at the Guinness head office in London's Portman Square, identified themselves as inspectors from the Department of Trade and Industry, and demanded to see a director of the company. The rumoured investigation was under way.

The press were on to it in a flash. Saunders's answer to the crisis was to deny everything. He denied that there was an investigation. He denied that an extraordinary board meeting had been scheduled. The game was up. Guinness' £100 million investment in the Boesky fund came to light.

Everyone was now minding their own back. Tom Ward scuttled back to America and never returned. Roger Seelig resigned from Morgan Grenfell and retained top people's solicitor Sir David Napley. On 5 January 1987, Napley received a letter from Olivier Roux in which the Frenchman admitted his part in the illegal share-support scheme, and named Saunders as the main protagonist. Napley sent a copy of the letter to Saunders and his fellow directors.

Saunders must have known he was finished. But he elected to bluff it out to the end, fending off Sir Norman Macfarlane's demands that he resign. By 14 January, however, Macfarlane and the board had had enough. They sacked Saunders without pay or benefits, and left him to face his accusers alone.

SLUSH FUND

The new Guinness board retained accountants Price Waterhouse, and it didn't take them long to unearth evidence of the share-support scheme.

There were mysterious invoices for 'advice and services' totalling £25 million. Among the recipients of this slush fund were Sir Jack Lyons, Anthony Parnes and Gerald Ronson.

Then Gerald Ronson repaid more than £5 million to Guinness, saying that he had been an unwitting pawn in the scheme. Like Olivier Roux, he pointed the finger at Saunders. Saunders, now under siege from the press, sought refuge at his ski chalet in Switzerland. Meanwhile Price Waterhouse and the Guinness accountants were trying to trace the whereabouts of the rest of the £25 million slush fund.

Over £5 million was eventually traced to a mysterious firm of consultants with a bank account in Jersey, a company which transpired to be the property of Tom Ward. Another £3 million had spent some time in Saunders's personal account in Switzerland before being handed over to Sir Jack Lyons.

IVAN BOESKY WAS OFFERED A DEAL BY THE US AUTHORITIES. THE BIG QUESTION ON WALL STREET WAS: WHO WOULD HE TAKE DOWN WITH HIM?

Below: ***Saunders was left financially destitute by the legal proceedings.***

On 5 May, at the insistence of his lawyers, Saunders returned to England to face DTI inspectors. Barely had he set foot in the country than he was arrested by officers of the Fraud Squad.

He spent the night at Holborn police station and the following morning appeared at Bow Street Magistrates' Court. There he was charged with intent to pervert the course of justice, and the destruction and falsification of documents.

Bail was set at £500,000. 'Tiny' Rowland came up with half the money. Saunders's family and friends deposited the rest.

On 1 October, Anthony Parnes was arrested at Los Angeles airport and spent the next six months in Terminal Island prison fighting extradition before returning to England voluntarily. Later in October Sir Jack Lyons, Gerald Ronson and Roger Seelig were all arrested.

TWO TRIALS

At the remand hearing in April 1989, Mr Justice Henry stated that the case was so cumbersome that there would be two trials. The first would examine the charges against Lyons, Parnes and Ronson.

In February 1990, after a year of pre-trial hearings, the trial finally got under way at the specially converted Southwark Crown Court. The Old Bailey had been too small to house the army of barristers and solicitors, not to mention the tons of paperwork.

Some of the original charges had been dropped to make the trial more manageable and comprehensible to the jury. Saunders and the other defendants now faced a total of twenty-four charges.

The question before the court was not if the share-support scheme had happened – it patently had – but rather who had engineered it and who had known about it. All four pleaded not guilty on all counts, and proceeded to try and shift the responsibility on to their former colleagues.

Ronson blamed Parnes. Parnes blamed Saunders. Lyons was an honest lobbyist who claimed that he had no idea that anything illegal was going on. And Saunders continued with his tactic of denying everything.

The most damaging evidence against Saunders came in the form of a statement by his erstwhile right-hand man, Olivier Roux. Roux had been granted immunity from prosecution in exchange for his cooperation. He said that Saunders had personally authorized all illegal payments, except one to Ronson. Saunders's barrister attempted to discredit this evidence, saying that Roux was a desperate man lying to save his own skin.

There were fourteen weeks of mind-bogglingly complex financial evidence before Ernest Saunders finally took the stand. He continued to insist that he was the only member of the Guinness board who was telling the truth, calling the testimony of his co-defendants 'bullshit'.

Saunders's cross-examination by the prosecution QC, John Chadwick, lasted eight days and painted the defendant as pananoid, arrogant and inconsistent.

The jury retired for six days before returning their verdict. They decided to a man that Ernest Saunders was a crook, and so were his three co-defendants.

On the following day, 27 August 1990, Mr Justice Henry passed sentence. He gave Saunders five years for conspiracy and three and a half years for false accounting, the two sentences to run concurrently. Anthony Parnes collapsed as he heard the judge order him to prison for two and a half years.

Gerald Ronson was up next. Mr Justice Henry described his participation in the share-support scheme as 'an aberrant moment of greed in an otherwise exemplary life', and then handed down a one-year prison sentence and a fine of £5 million, the biggest in British legal history.

Sir Jack Lyons was spared a prison sentence because of his age and ill health, but was fined £3 million for his part in the fraud. All the defendants with the exception of Saunders, who was now financially destitute, were ordered to pay £440,000 costs. In his summing-up, Mr Justice Henry said: 'When men are hell-bent on victory, greed is in the saddle and normal commercial probity and respect for the law are thrust aside.'

SAUNDERS CONTINUED TO INSIST THAT HE WAS THE ONLY MEMBER OF THE BOARD TELLING THE TRUTH, CALLING THE TESTIMONY OF HIS CO-DEFENDANTS 'BULLSHIT'

HOWARD MARKS
Cannabis King

Like many of his sixties' contemporaries, Oxford graduate Howard Marks started dope dealing in a small way. By the time of his arrest in 1988 he was running a huge international drug empire and had been involved with both MI6 and the IRA

Above: ***The Marks family's villa in Palma de Mallorca.***

Opposite: ***Tipped for a brilliant career, Howard Marks achieved his ambition to 'make a million pounds' by very different means.***

In many ways, Howard Marks could not have been less like his counterparts in the Latin American cocaine cartels, or the inscrutable heroin dealers from the Golden Triangle. He was an intelligent, witty and urbane university graduate who loathed hard drugs and despised violence.

Left: ***Howard's wife Judy, sister of his 'accountant', Patrick Lane.***

ASKED BY HIS OXFORD TUTOR WHAT HIS AMBITIONS WERE, MARKS REPLIED: 'MAKE A MILLION POUNDS. BE FAMOUS. GET SOMEWHERE.'

Yet in the 1970s and 1980s he rose to control one of Europe's most powerful drug trafficking organizations, and became the target of the US Drug Enforcement Agency's most extensive and costly investigation.

Born to a middle-class family in South Wales, Marks won a scholarship to Balliol, one of Oxford University's most prestigious colleges. Everyone who knew Howard expected great things of him, and indeed he expected great things of himself. Asked by his tutor what his ambitions were, he answered: 'Make a million pounds. Be famous. Get somewhere.'

DROP-OUTS AND DOPE

After leaving Oxford, he was at a loose end. Marks, who had smoked dope – hashish and marijuana – since his early days at Oxford, started dealing on a small scale. Then he sold cannabis for his friend Graham Plinston, an Oxford contemporary who had been rusticated for drugs offences.

Plinston was dealing on a considerable scale and, while Marks was strictly an amateur at this stage, he was already getting a taste for the business. It wasn't just the money that attracted him. It was also the excitement and intrigue.

In 1969 Marks and his girlfriend Ilse moved down to Brighton. He enrolled at Sussex University on the pretext of doing a doctorate. In fact, he spent most of his time drinking and peddling Graham Plinston's dope around the pubs of Brighton.

Soon his relationship with Ilse collapsed and he started an affair with Rosie Brindley, the beautiful wife of a Sussex University maths lecturer. She too was an avid cannabis fan and thoroughly approved of Howard's lifestyle.

MOVING UP THE LADDER

Howard and Rosie moved back to London in 1970 and rented a mews house in Ladbroke Grove, from which Howard continued to sell dope for Plinston. Marks wasn't cut out to be anyone's dogsbody, however, and he was determined to become a dealer in his own right.

His opportunity came a few months later when he received a frantic call from Plinston's girlfriend. Graham was missing. He had been on a buying trip in Germany and was now three days overdue.

Despite never having been abroad before, Marks volunteered to fly to Germany and sort things out. He was met in Frankfurt by one of Plinston's associates and was alarmed to discover that his friend had been arrested on the Swiss border with 100lb of hashish hidden in the door panels of his car.

Marks arranged for a lawyer to handle Plinston's defence and flew back to London. On Howard's return, Plinston's girl had another job for him. Would he meet up with Graham's Middle East contacts and straighten them out?

The foreign dealers suggested that Howard take the job as their London distributor while Plinston was incapacitated. Marks readily accepted.

Plinston, released a few weeks later after serving a token jail sentence, scuttled back to London. He was badly shaken by his experience, however, and started to delegate most of his overseas work to Marks. As the months passed, their dope shipments got bigger and more frequent and the money began pouring in.

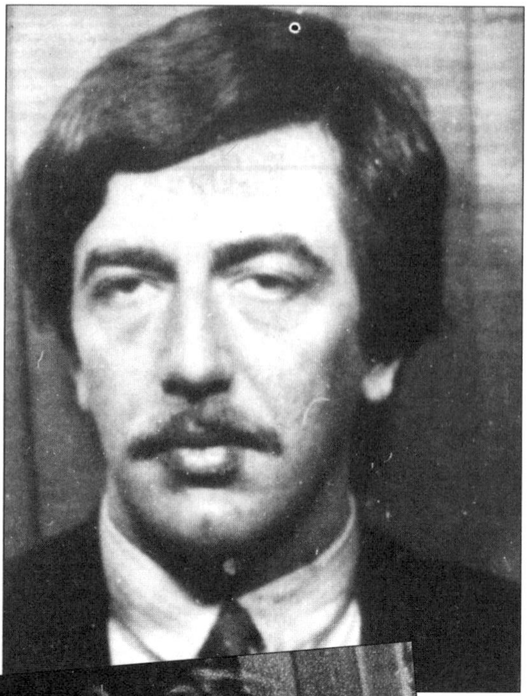

Right and below: ***Two of the disguises used by Howard Marks.***

DESPERATE MEASURES

These halcyon days came to an abrupt halt in the summer of 1971 when their supply of cannabis dried up. One of their suppliers, 'Mike' Durrani, placed the ball firmly in their court. He had a contact in Karachi who could get the dope out and into the air, but it was up to Plinston and Marks to find a way to land it.

They were having lunch one day with a young South African publisher, Alan Marcuson, and were discussing their dilemma. Marcuson told them that he had a friend who could arrange for shipments to be landed. His name was Jim McCann and he lived in Ireland.

Both Marks and Plinston took Marcuson's story with a pinch of salt. But by the autumn of 1971 their business had effectively ground to a halt, cash was running low, and their customers were defecting to other suppliers.

Marcuson arranged for them to meet McCann in Ballinskelligs, Co. Kerry. McCann, in his early thirties, was a drunk and a braggart, and both men instinctively mistrusted him. Despite their reservations, however, Marks and Plinston decided to put McCann to the test.

If nothing else, McCann had nerve and cunning. Posing as a journalist, he contacted the manager of Shannon Airport and told him that his publication was conducting a survey of airports for an upcoming edition on air freight. He was duly given the VIP treatment as he toured the place, and left Shannon with an armful of maps and diagrams together with a pile of blank customs dockets.

Marks and Plinston were impressed when McCann went on to tell them that he had persuaded one of the customs men to turn a blind eye if dockets arrived out of sequence. 'I told him I was with the IRA and led him to believe that the shipments were arms for the boys in the North,' McCann explained.

WELL-LAUNDERED FROCKS

Marks, Plinston and McCann set about testing the system. Their first shipment, 200lb of hashish from Karachi, was

Below: ***Howard Marks and his wife Judy.***

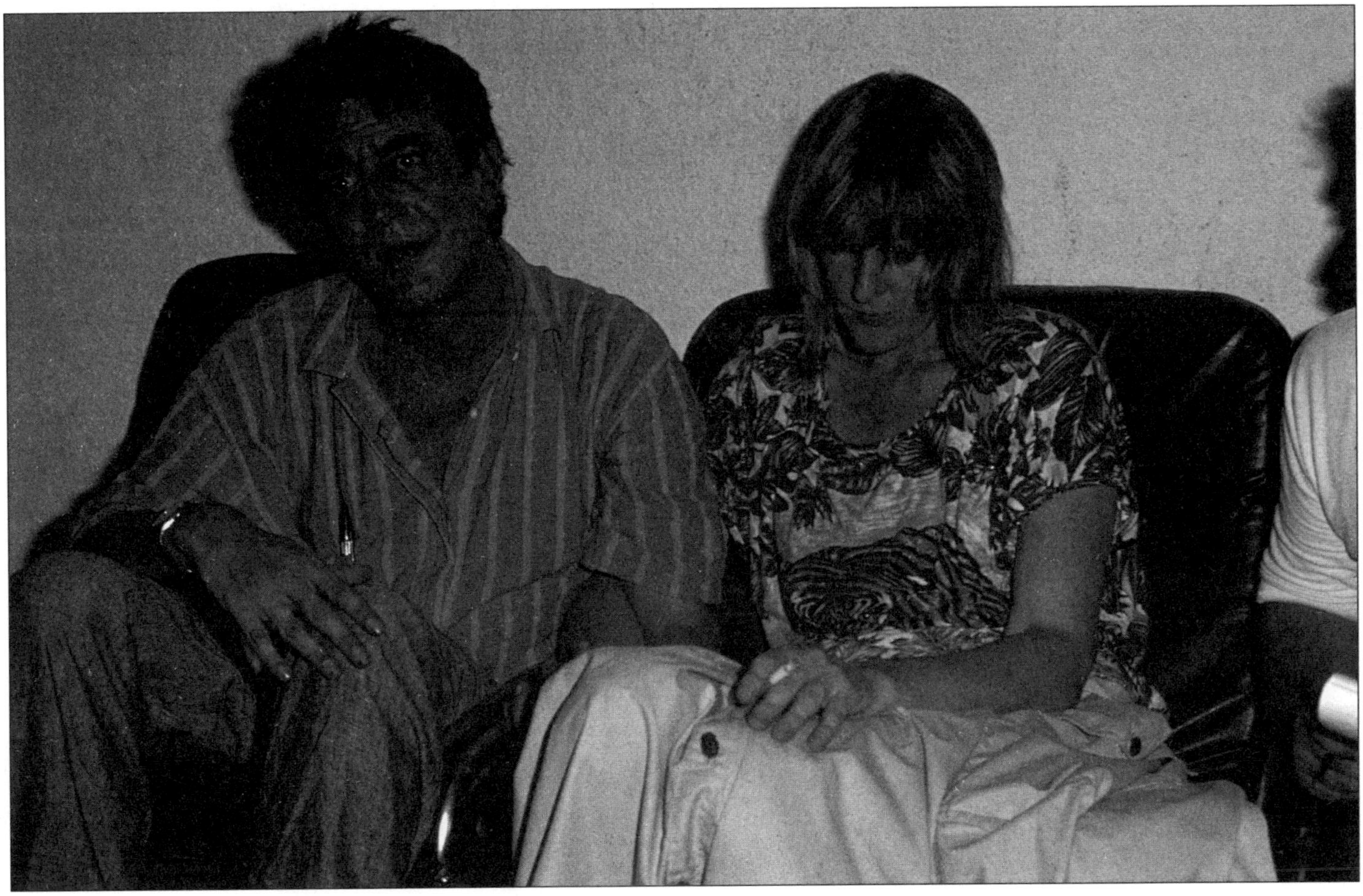

cleared without a hitch. It was shipped back to England under the back seat of Plinston's car.

The second shipment was a whole ton, and Marks had put together a team to transport the dope back to England. The drivers were mainly young, poorly paid Oxford graduates who were happy to take a risk for a fee which exceeded their annual income.

The McCann arrangement went sour when he started bullying Marks's drivers into running guns for the IRA

The Shannon scam continued to work flawlessly for two years, during which time the partnership brought in more than ten tons of hashish. The profits were staggering. Marks alone was clearing in excess of $50,000 a ton, and he established a number of business 'fronts' to explain away his lavish lifestyle.

One of these was a dress shop in Oxford called Annabelinda. Marks, however, kept control of the accounts. Over the next few years the shop generated huge profits, as Marks laundered his drug profits through Annabelinda's books.

GOING TRANSATLANTIC

By the end of 1973, despite its success, the Shannon partnership was beginning to pall. Jim McCann was becoming a liability. He was now living in Amsterdam, under the name Jim O'Neill, and was claiming to be an adjutant in the IRA. He was stealing from Plinston and Marks and was trying to bully Marks's drivers into running guns for him.

Plinston went to America to investigate the possibility of going intercontinental. While he was there he met

Below: ***The many faces of Howard Marks.***

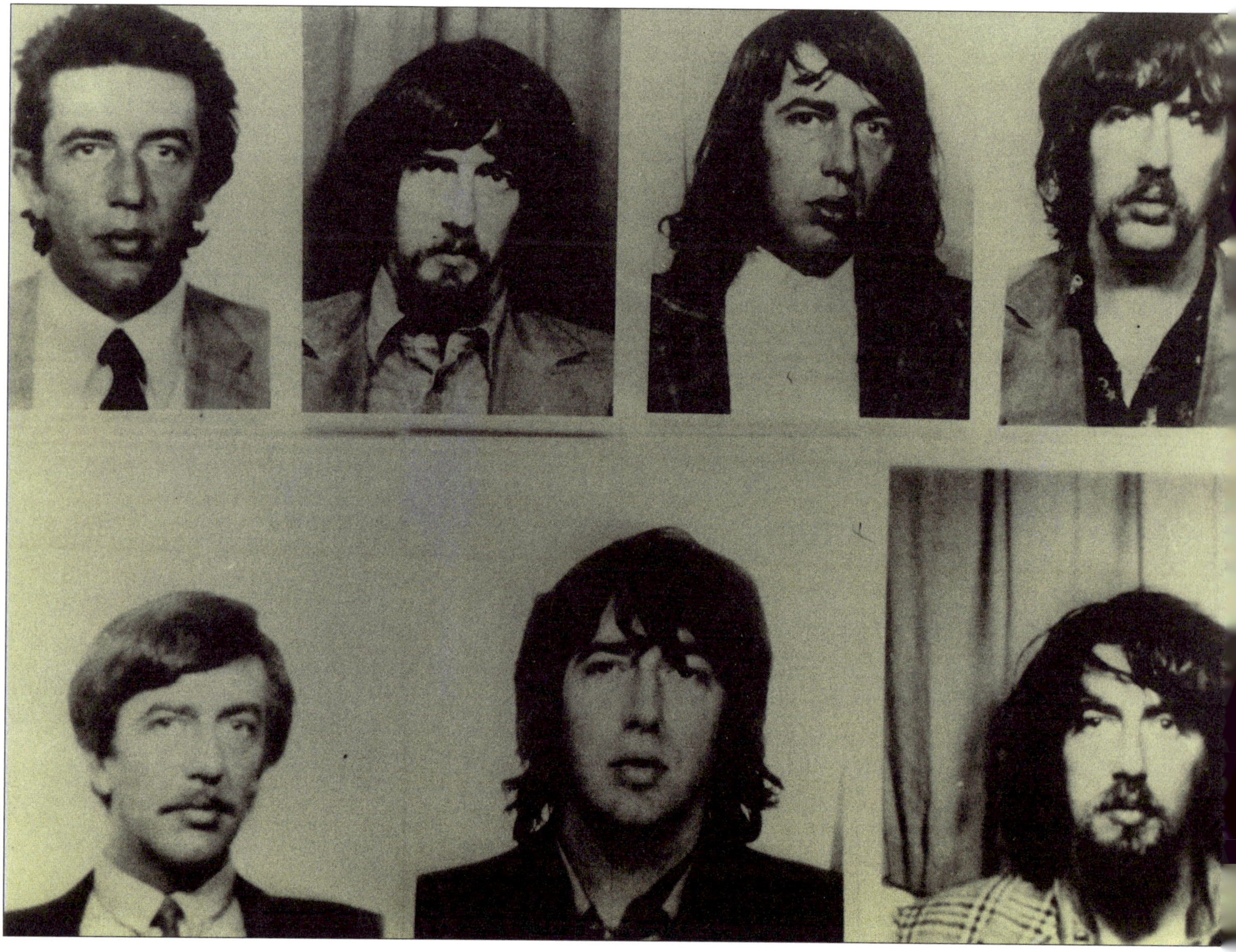

Ernie 'Peter' Combs, a big-time Californian dope dealer.

Combs was sick of dealing in marijuana; it was too bulky and, because of the huge amount of home-grown available on the West Coast, the price had slipped. His customers were crying out for top-grade cannabis. Plinston assured him that he and Marks could guarantee him a regular supply if they could find a way of getting it into the country.

The three men considered several possibilities before involving a friend of Combs's, a 'roadie' called Jim Morris. He was constantly moving huge shipments of freight in and out of the United States through a scheme called 'ATA Carnets', which meant his equipment was treated as a temporary import and virtually exempt from customs.

By the autumn of 1972 they were ready to move. Plinston and Marks hid half a ton of cannabis in thirty speaker cabinets which Morris then shipped to California. Here they were collected without any difficulty by Ernie Combs.

RECRUITED BY MI6

In December 1972, Marks returned to Oxford where he had set up house with Rosie Brindley and their daughter. When he popped into Annabelinda, he found an old friend waiting for him.

Hamilton 'Mac' McMillan and Marks had been close at Balliol, but they had not seen one another since graduation. Without being specific, he gave Marks the impression that his work was connected with intelligence. Marks had a distinct feeling that Mac's visit had not been purely social.

A few days later, his curiosity aroused, Marks paid Mac a visit at his home in the London suburb of Putney. This time Mac dropped all pretence. He was in fact working for the British Intelligence Service and wondered if Marks had ever thought of 'helping...that sort of thing'.

Marks, a born fantasist, jumped at the opportunity to be a real live spy. McMillan explained that there were several Soviet agents working in London under the guise of junior diplomats. There was a young woman working at the Czech Embassy who was suspected of espionage. Marks's job would be to compromise her sexually. But the assignation never materialized. The girl in question failed to turn up at the party where Marks was meant to pick her up. Mac was deeply embarrassed by the fiasco, but Marks shrugged it off. 'Don't worry, some other time.'

A few days later, Mac appeared again and put a business proposition to Marks. If MI6 backed him, would Marks be prepared to open a branch of Annabelinda in Amsterdam and allow it to be used as a front by British Intelligence?

This was simply too good to be true. MI6 were offering to sponsor Marks to establish a legitimate business cover in the drugs capital of Europe. Needless to say, he accepted Mac's offer.

MI6 now had their hooks into Marks. A few weeks later, he was summoned by Mac to meet his boss, 'Donald'. Now, for the first time, he began to understand the relevance of Amsterdam and why he had been selected for the assignment.

British Intelligence, Donald explained, were on to a gang of arms dealers operating out of Amsterdam who were

Above: ***Everyone who knew Howard Marks expected great things of him, and indeed he expected great things of himself.***

Above: ***Howard Marks.***

To his embarrassment, Marks was asked by British Intelligence to 'shop' his former partner Jim McCann

'Hey, one of you guys out there. You just lost five million dollars!'

supplying the IRA in Northern Ireland. The ringleader was one James O'Neill. They knew that O'Neill was a friend of Marks's and they wanted him to find out what he could about dates and movements of arms shipments.

Marks was horrified. He knew James O'Neill all right. It was the alias adopted by his erstwhile partner Jim McCann.

He decided to duck the problem for a while and flew to Ibiza where Rosie Brindley, sick of Marks and the dope business, had set up home with her children. Marks made a half-hearted attempt at a reconciliation, but Marks's ever-roving eye soon fell on seventeen-year-old Judy Lane, younger sister of Plinston's 'accountant' Patrick Lane.

Marks spent the rest of the summer travelling around Europe, doing deals and shifting money. In September he found himself back in Amsterdam and decided to make a show of helping MI6. So he called Mac in London.

He got an icy reception. McMillan told him that his department was no longer prepared to use the criminal element as agents, and that Marks should never call him again.

BUSTED

In the autumn of 1973, business had never been better for the Marks-Plinston partnership. Shipments were moving to Combs in California at a rate of one a month, at a net profit of £50,000 per load to Marks.

On 13 September, the day after his rebuff from McMillan, Marks flew out to California. A huge shipment of drugs was due to be landed in Las Vegas.

The following morning, he switched on the television and saw a reporter staring at him from the screen and announcing cheerily: 'Hey, one of you guys out there. You just lost five million dollars!' The camera pulled back and revealed a stack of huge speakers with their backs ripped off.

Marks didn't know whether the American authorities had any evidence to connect him with the shipment, but he wasn't about to hang around and find out. Within minutes, he was out of the hotel and heading for the airport. He flew back to Britain and lay low in London for several months.

Once he considered it safe, he travelled to Amsterdam. Marks was paying a social visit to an old friend, Arend ter Host, when the house was raided by Dutch police. They arrested Host and, as a matter of routine, searched Marks. When they found him to be carrying a small quantity of hashish, they locked him up for the night.

The following morning, Marks found himself confronted by two British customs officials, Mark Elliot and Robin Eynon. They questioned him for ten hours, and they weren't interested in the few grams of hash for which he had just been arrested. They were after much bigger things.

At first Howard denied everything. Then, as it became obvious that the two customs men knew all about the Las Vegas bust and had a great deal of hard evidence, he changed tack.

He told Elliot and Eynon that he was only a pawn in the drug ring and that he was in reality working for British Intelligence. The customs men had heard it all before. They shipped him back to England where he was sent to Brixton Prison. Elliot and Eynon appeared in court to object to bail. But, against all the odds, Marks was released on a bond of £50,000.

On 2 May 1974, a week before he was due to stand trial at the Old Bailey, Marks disappeared, apparently abducted from his Oxford digs. The fact is that Howard had faked his own abduction and was in hiding on the Isle of Dogs in London's East End. A few weeks later he travelled to Italy on a false passport in the name of McKenna.

In the autumn he travelled to New York, this time with Judy Lane. Far from keeping a low profile in America, the couple were to be seen swanning around Manhattan in stretch limos, dining at fashionable restaurants and dancing at Regine's or Studio 54.

When winter came, Howard and Judy moved south to Florida and rented a house in Key Biscayne. There they met up with Ernie Combs and went back into business, shipping huge quantities of hashish into the United States.

THE 'GREAT BIG MONSTER DEAL'

In October 1977, three years after his escape, Marks returned to London where Judy gave birth to their first daughter, Amber. Far from retiring, Howard Marks continued his association with Combs and now planned the biggest dope deal of his career.

On 29 December 1979, 15 tons of Colombian hashish – enough for a joint for every man, woman and child in Britain – was landed on the west coast of Scotland. It was Marks's 'great big monster deal'.

But things did not go well. The market soon became saturated and stocks were slow to move. Then, in January, some of the consignment was discovered in Scotland by the police.

In May 1980, Marks took Judy and Amber for a holiday in East Anglia. He was alone in the bar of the Swan Hotel at Lavenham when Nicholas Baker, executive officer of Her Majesty's Customs, slipped a pair of handcuffs on to his wrists and led him away. Two days later, Marks was back in Brixton Prison. This time there was no question of bail.

In October 1981, eighteen months after his arrest, Marks's trial finally began at the Old Bailey. Marks took the stand and told the jury fantastic stories of his work for MI6 and their fight against IRA terrorism. He admitted that he had been involved in smuggling activities – but these, he claimed, were merely a cover for his espionage activities.

John Rogers, cross-examining, made a fatal error when he conceded that Marks had indeed worked for British Intelligence at one time. The prosecution was now in real trouble. Since MI6 did not officially exist, they could hardly send a representative to court to refute

ARRESTED BY BRITISH CUSTOMS FOR THE LAS VEGAS DRUGS HAUL, MARKS CLAIMED IT WAS PART OF HIS MI6 COVER

Below: ***In December 1979, Marks landed 15 tons of Colombian hashish on the west coast of Scotland. But shortly afterwards, much of the cargo was discovered hidden in the loft of a house at Glengarry.***

Above: ***The ocean-going tug aboard which the 15 tons of hashish were shipped to Scotland.***

SINCE MI6 DID NOT OFFICIALLY EXIST, THE PROSECUTION COULD NOT CALL ON ITS MEMBERS TO TESTIFY AGAINST MARKS

Marks's claims. On 20 November the jury reached a verdict. Howard Marks walked out of the Old Bailey a free man.

THE POTTY PEER

Marks spent the next couple of years based in England. He was in the process of building up two quasi-legitimate businesses – a travel agency and a language school – with offices strategically placed in Karachi, Bangkok and Hong Kong.

In April 1984, the Marks family moved to Majorca. Within months, huge shipments of cannabis began to appear on the West Coast of the United States. Howard Marks and Ernie Combs were back in business.

Marks spent the next two years travelling widely – Pakistan, Hong Kong and the Philippines – setting up deals and moving money about. But, unknown to him, the American DEA in the person of Madrid-based Craig Lovato were on to him and his organization. They had a tap on his phone and were tracking his movements across the world.

What the DEA wanted was for someone to betray Howard Marks, and they had just the man in mind.

One of Marks's closest associates in the Philippines was Lord 'Tony' Moynihan, an enforced exile from Great Britain where he was wanted on fraud charges. In 1986, however, Moynihan's exit visa was revoked and he found himself under virtual house arrest.

The DEA knew all about Moynihan and his dealings with Howard Marks, and decided to capitalize on the 'potty peer's' misfortune. In July 1987, Craig Lovato flew out to Manila and offered Moynihan a deal. 'Give us Marks and we'll give you immunity from prosecution in the Unites States.' Lovato gave Moynihan the night to think it over. In the morning, they met again. 'All right,' Moynihan said. 'What do I have to do?' 'Go see

Howard,' Lovato said,'and wear a wire.'

Three months later, Moynihan and Marks met up in Barcelona and travelled back to Howard's villa in Majorca together. Over the next week they talked as friends and colleagues will talk. They talked about deals. They talked about mutual friends. They talked about money. All these conversations were recorded and would form the basis for the DEA's case against Marks.

In July 1988, Craig Lovato appeared before a grand jury to summarize his case against the Marks organization. Arrest warrants were issued against twenty-two of Howard Marks's associates in Canada, Britain, the Netherlands, Pakistan, Thailand and Spain. Back in Majorca, Lovato watched the Marks villa for a few days. Then, on 25 July, with the help of the Spanish police, he arrested both Howard and Judy Marks at gunpoint.

MARKS WAS TOO CLEVER TO GIVE HIMSELF AWAY – WHAT THE DEA NEEDED WAS FOR AN ASSOCIATE TO GIVE HIM AWAY

THE MARKS EMPIRE COLLAPSES

From a cell in Alcala Meco high-security prison near Madrid, Marks watched the collapse of his empire. His main concern was to avoid extradition to the United States, where he would face charges under draconian racketeering laws. Marks's English lawyer, Michael Katz, suggested he plead guilty to offences in Spain, under whose laws he need expect only a fraction of the American sentence.

Below: ***Howard Marks, the intelligent, witty and urbane university graduate who loathed hard drugs and despised violence.***

It was a good idea. But the Spaniards ignored his confession and, in March 1989, granted the US authorities' request for extradition. Katz lodged an appeal.

While Marks awaited the outcome of his appeal, he received the depressing news that his friend and colleague Ernie Combs had been sentenced to forty years without parole. In contrast Patrick Lane, Marks's brother-in-law and accountant, had got off lightly with three years.

Marks's appeal was finally rejected. On 22 October 1989, he was put on a TWA flight for New York, handcuffed to two US marshals. After a couple of weeks in Miami's Metropolitan Correction Centre he was transferred to North Dade Detention Centre, and started to work on preparing a defence.

He decided to admit to smuggling drugs to Britain, Spain, Canada – anywhere except the United States.

The DEA knew Howard Marks' remarkable history and were taking no chances on him pulling off a court room coup like he had done at the Old Bailey. They approached both Combs and Lane and, by a combination of threats and inducements, tried to coerce them into testifying against Marks.

Both men eventually weakened. When he was shown their testimony, Marks knew the game was up. He was told by the DEA that if he pleaded guilty he could expect a sentence of forty years. If he didn't, they'd go for the maximum – a hundred years without parole.

On 13 July 1990 Howard Marks appeared in court in West Palm Beach, Florida. He pleaded guilty to one charge of racketeering and another of conspiracy to smuggle drugs into the United States.

The question of Marks's sentence was a matter of intense and very public debate. The DEA considered that his offences were at least on a par with those of Combs and that he should therefore receive the same sentence – forty years.

Marks's family and friends, however, lobbied the court and probation office. He was not, they insisted, a vicious criminal. In the end, Judge Paine settled on a compromise, sentencing Marks to twenty-five years.

JOHN DE LOREAN
Whizzkid Conman

Ex-General Motors whizzkid John De Lorean dreamed of manufacturing the perfect 'ethical car'. But the truth revealed a highly unethical lifestyle for this big-time con artist and cocaine dealer

Left: ***When he resigned from the board of General Motors in 1972, John De Lorean set himself up as a consultant.***

Opposite: ***He captured the public imagination with his flamboyant lifestyle and trendy dress.***

THE PUBLICITY-HUNGRY DE LOREAN'S TASTES WERE JUST TOO FLASHY FOR THE SOBER SUITS AT GM

In the late afternoon of 19 October 1982, FBI agent Gerry West burst into a Los Angeles motel room and placed a suave middle-aged businessman under arrest. The charge was conspiring to buy and distribute more than $100 million worth of narcotics; the man was John Zachary De Lorean.

The world's press was astonished, not by the size of the drug deal but by the identity of the accused. John De Lorean was a household name, perhaps the most flamboyant entrepreneur of his day. De Lorean had captured the public's imagination by taking on the world's automotive industry and apparently

Below: ***De Lorean at the wheel of the so-called 'ethical' car in 1981.***

Above: ***In 1985, a weary-looking De Lorean faced arraignment on racketeering charges.***

winning. What was a man of his ilk doing trafficking cocaine? It simply didn't make sense.

Gradually, however, it became clear that the De Lorean myth was just that – a myth based on lies, deceit, fraud and outright theft. In a period of six years, the De Lorean organization had milked almost £200 million from the British government, and John De Lorean's foray into the drugs world appeared to be a desperate last attempt to cover their tracks.

OUT OF THE FAST LANE

The De Lorean saga really begins in 1972 when John De Lorean inexplicably resigned from the board of General Motors, the world's biggest car manufacturers.

At the time GM were predictably tight-lipped on the subject. Unofficial versions of the resignation, however, suggest that, rather than jumping, De Lorean might have been pushed from the fourteenth floor of GM's Detroit headquarters.

WHEN A CUSTOMER'S PROJECT INEXPLICABLY CAUGHT FIRE IT WAS DE LOREAN WHO POCKETED THE INSURANCE HAND-OUT

His style, in both his personal and business life, might just have been a bit too flashy. His taste for the high life, his psuedo-hippy philosophy and trendy clothes, his divorce and subsequent marriage to a teenage model did not sit well with the ultra-conservative GM bosses.

Freed from corporate constraints, De Lorean announced his intention of taking the automotive world head on by producing a so-called 'ethical' car. Even De Lorean realized that this dream would take time and money to achieve.

De Lorean's first move was to set up his own company, the John Z. De Lorean Corporation and to announce himself in business as a consultant.

De Lorean's years of self-publicity now paid off, and he soon had a list of prestigious clients including Allstate Insurance, W.R. Grace, Renault and Piper Aircraft. In its first two years, the consultancy made a profit of approximately $5 million. A success, one might say, until one looks at what the clients actually got for their money.

Allstate, for instance, paid De Lorean about £1 million to develop prototypes for an air-bag safety system and an economy commuter car. Neither project ever got off the drawing board, and Allstate received no refund on their investment. Likewise, W.R. Grace paid De Lorean £1 million to develop an economical recreational vehicle.

At least this project got to prototype stage, but the prototype mysteriously caught fire one night and was totally destroyed. It had been insured for $100,000 and when the claim was met, the money was not returned to the client but pocketed by the John Z. De Lorean Corporation.

The list of business failures in which he was directly or indirectly involved during this period is seemingly endless. There was Grand Prix of America, a chain of miniature racing circuits; there was a failed ranch, a bankrupt car dealership, a disputed engine coolant system, and a warehouse full of defective CB radios.

However, far from being destroyed by his failures, John De Lorean emerged smelling of roses.

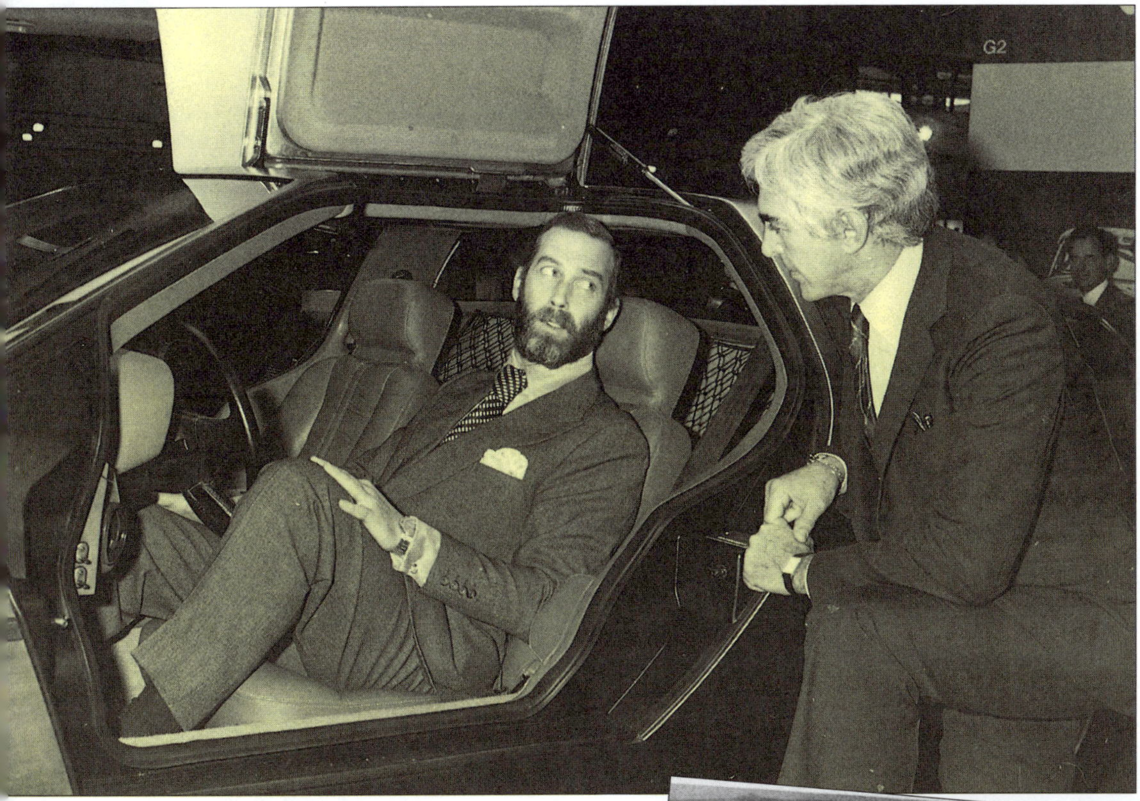

Left: ***Prince Michael of Kent discusses the revolutionary car with its manufacturer.***

IN LESS THAN EIGHTEEN MONTHS DMC'S WORKING CAPITAL HAD RISEN TO $6 MILLION — WITHOUT A PROTOTYPE IN SIGHT

A COMPANY IS BORN

The De Lorean Motor Company (DMC) was formed in the autumn of 1975, funded almost entirely by John De Lorean's unwitting consultancy clients. According to press releases, DMC would develop and produce a revolutionary sports car. It was to be called the De Lorean-12, was to be built in an ultra-light space-age plastic (ERM) and have the gull-wing doors made famous by Mercedes in the 1950s.

Without even producing a prototype, De Lorean set about raising more working capital. He issued shares and partnerships in DMC and, in less than eighteen months, increased its working capital by $6 million.

Car development is expensive at the best of times, and in DMC's case the situation was not helped by John De Lorean's personal extravagance. The money was running out fast, and what DMC really needed was a single investor to come up with about $80 million.

Governments, he reasoned, were the answer to the problem. De Lorean spent the next year jetting around trying to set up deals with government and state development boards. Again he was well received and by 1978 he had offers from the states of Michigan, Ohio and Rhode Island, together with two Canadian provinces and the governments of Spain, the Republic of Ireland and Puerto Rico.

Then, out of the blue, he received a call from the British Labour government in the form of NIDA, the Northern Ireland Development Board. Desperate to create employment in the war-torn province, NIDA's offer to De Lorean was truly astonishing.

The whole deal was worth $97 million, of which $20 million was an outright

Above: ***De Lorean attempts to explain away his financial troubles to the press.***

grant. De Lorean would retain 73 per cent of the voting stock in the company for a personal investment of a mere $1 million. Six weeks after NIDA first called De Lorean, the deal was signed.

FAIRY GODMOTHER: HER MAJESTY'S GOVERNMENT

John De Lorean had a real chance now of making his dream car a reality, but he started to dream up ways to syphon some of the money off for his personal use. His solution to this dilemma was hardly subtle.

On the morning of 18 October 1978, a junior executive of DMC's New York office was instructed to take a cab down to the Wall Street branch of the Chemical Bank and draw a cheque in the name of GPD Services in the amount of $12.5 million. GPD was a Panamanian-registered company with a bank account in Switzerland. It only ever had one employee, a Mrs Marie-Denise Juhan, yet over the next year DMC paid GPD a total of $17.76 million — money that has never been accounted for.

How did a Panamanian-registered company with a single employee receive nearly $18 million from DMC?

Asked about the payments, De Lorean explained that GPD was an engineering consultancy which was helping to develop the prototype of the De Lorean-12. The fact is that De Lorean not only had Bill Collins and his design team, but they had also sub-contracted design work to Lotus Cars Ltd and the legendary Colin Chapman.

De Lorean then claimed that GPD had acted as a middleman at Colin Chapman's insistence so that he, Chapman, could avoid Britain's punitive taxes. Lotus were indeed paid a total of $24 million for their work, but this money came direct from Belfast. Not a penny came from GPD.

What happened to the money remains a mystery. No one in the company, however, believed that De Lorean would be brazen enough to steal so vast a sum of money. In the words of Walter Strycker, GMC's then financial controller: 'It would be such a goddam stupid thing to do, we just couldn't believe John would have done it.'

Below: ***A grim John De Lorean and his attorney arrive at the Los Angeles court to face charges of cocaine dealing.***

EXAGGERATED CLAIMS

To say that De Lorean's production forecasts were ambitious would be a masterpiece of understatement. He had promised NIDA that the car would be in pilot production in twenty months and that full production — thirty thousand

cars per annum – would start the following year.

This was totally unrealistic. Despite all these problems, De Lorean seldom visited Belfast. He hated the city and was afraid of being kidnapped by the IRA. Instead, he sat in regal splendour in New York, spending British taxpayers' money.

Above: ***By February 1982 unwanted De Lorean cars were piling up at the company's works in Belfast.***

Left: ***Colin Chapman, the boss of Lotus Cars Ltd, agreed that his company would carry out some of the design work on the new car.***

All in all the New York operation, three thousand miles from the Belfast factory, was costing DMC more than $8 million a year. Some of this expenditure was no more than corporate irresponsibility; but some was later construed as blatant fraud.

Soon the money ran out, and in September 1980 De Lorean browbeat an additional loan of $33 million out of NIDA. Two months later he was back again. This time he managed to persuade them to guarantee loans of an additional $40 million. The British government's investment in DMC, direct and indirect, had thus spiralled to $160 million, and not a single car had yet been produced.

On 21 January 1981, the first De Lorean-12 finally limped off the assembly line in Belfast. It looked quite sleek, but none met the criteria for safety, fuel consumption, price or performance which De Lorean had still been boasting about six months earlier.

Despite its shortcomings, the De Lorean-12 initially took off in a big way, and by the summer dealers could not keep up with demand. John De Lorean celebrated his apparent success by buying himself a 430-acre estate and mansion in New Jersey for $3.4 million. He also instructed his lawyer, Thomas Kimmerly to restructure DMC so that he, De Lorean, would be guaranteed maximum personal profit.

De Lorean would probably have got away with his plan if he could have sustained the public euphoria which surrounded him. But by the autumn of 1981 things were starting to turn sour. Sales of the De Lorean-12 were falling off, and stocks of unsold cars were piling up on the Belfast docks.

Questions about the wisdom of the British government's investment in DMC were being asked on both sides of the House of Commons. Before long the government announced an in-depth investigation into De Lorean's business conduct.

In September, trouble for De Lorean arrived in the form of Marian Gibson, his personal secretary and one-time office manager. She contacted Nicholas Winterton, a Conservative backbench

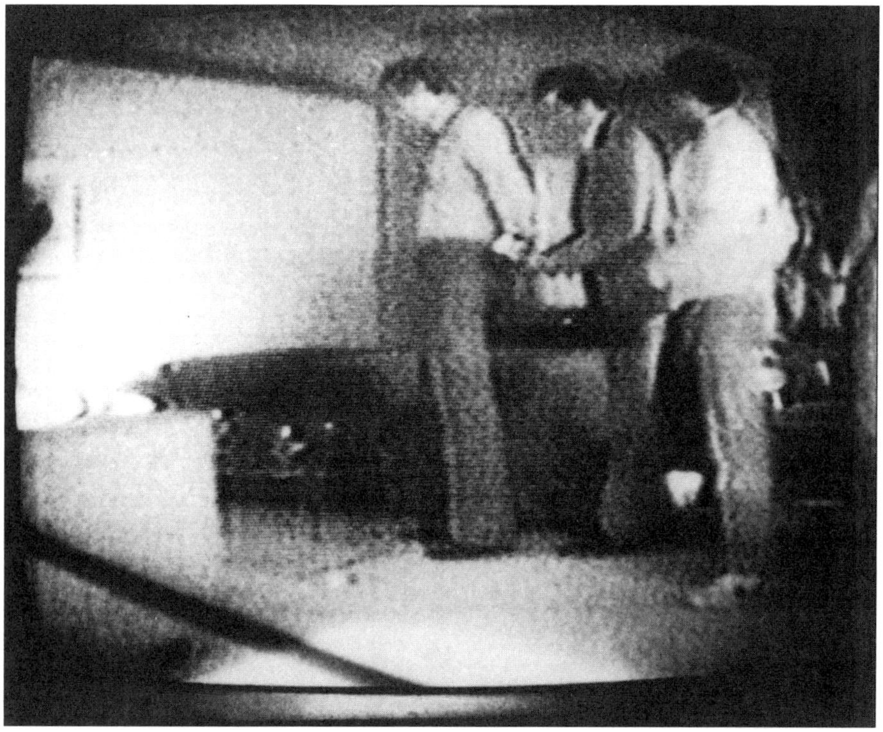

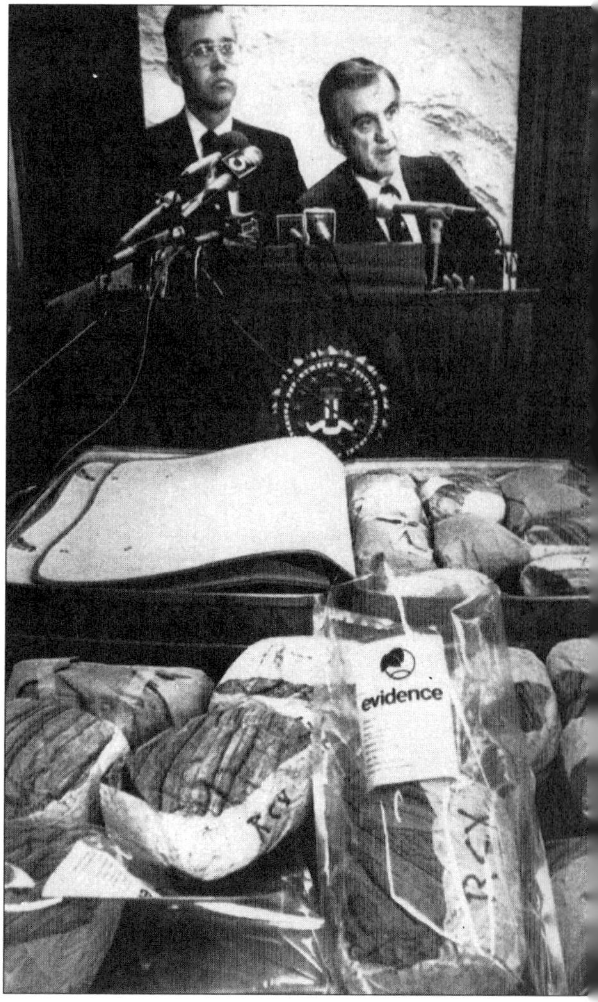

Above: ***A photograph from an FBI surveillance video, showing the arrest of John De Lorean for drug trafficking in Los Angeles in 1982.***

Right: ***Some 27 kilos of cocaine, said to be worth more than $24 million, were seized during the arrest.***

MP, saying that she had information of a most sensitive nature concerning the De Lorean Motor Company. Marian told of De Lorean's extravagant lifestyle, of money syphoned off from DMC to finance other De Lorean ventures.

Winterton studied the documentation and contacted Prime Minister Margaret Thatcher, who was on a trip to Australia. She immediately instructed the Attorney General, Sir Michael Havers, to start a police investigation into the allegations.

De Lorean decided to brazen the situation out. He flew into Heathrow the following day and told an army of reporters: 'I still can't understand how a troubled, nervous old typist and an MP never known for his intellectual clarity can cause so much trouble.'

But despite De Lorean's protestations of innocence, the damage was done. A share issue in New York was aborted. In London James Prior, Secretary of State for Northern Ireland, appointed Sir Kenneth Cork to evaluate the situation.

In February 1982, De Lorean was summoned to a meeting with Prior and Cork in London. Cork laid out his findings. The year 1981 had been a catastrophic one for DMC. The company had an operating loss of $23 million, and all the working capital was exhausted. There was, however, a way out.

WHEN HIS EX-SECRETARY SPILT THE BEANS, DE LOREAN SMOOTHLY DISMISSED HER TO THE PRESS AS A 'TROUBLED, NERVOUS OLD TYPIST'

Cork presented De Lorean with a complex restructuring package which involved the government writing off most of its investment. De Lorean for his part would have to invest $5 million of his own money. 'No trouble,' said De Lorean, 'I'll have the money in a few days.' With that John De Lorean jetted back to New York on Concorde.

In New York, things rapidly went from bad to worse for John De Lorean as he tried to persuade potential investors to finance his share of Kenneth Cork's rescue package. De Lorean's own behaviour became increasingly bizarre, vacillating between deep depression and unrealistic euphoria.

THE COCAINE DEAL IS SET UP

In San Diego, California, a separate drama was unfolding. James Timothy Hoffman, a big-time drug trafficker, had joined forces with the FBI. He and agent John Valestra were in the process of setting up cocaine dealer William Morgan Hetrick.

By sheer coincidence, Hoffman had once been a neighbour of John De Lorean, and Hetrick had been the private pilot to computer tycoon Fletcher Jones, one-time fiancé of a beautiful young model named Christina Ferrare, now Mrs John De Lorean.

Hoffman boasted of his friendship with De Lorean and, having heard about De Lorean's money troubles, suggested that he might be able to persuade him to become involved in the forthcoming drug deal with Hetrick. Valestra was sceptical

Hoffman contacted De Lorean and the two men met on 11 July at the Marriot Hotel in Newport Beach, California. Hoffman told De Lorean that he had some friends who might be interested in investing $15 million in DMC. If the deal went through, Hoffman would receive $1.8 million in commission.

De Lorean said he was interested in principle. He knew the deal involved drugs, but later claimed that he believed Hoffman intended to use his slice of the profits to buy drugs — not that he would be involved in anything illegal.

A few days later Hoffman and De Lorean met again in Washington, this time with Valestra, who posed as a Mafia dope dealer called Mr Vicenza. At the meeting, which was tape recorded, Vicenza offered to put up $3 million to De Lorean's $1.8 million to buy 100 kilos of Colombian cocaine. Hetrick would fly the drugs in from South America; Vicenza would handle the distribution; all John De Lorean would have to do was sit back and pick up $15 million for his efforts.

While the deal was going through, the US authorities tipped off the British government that De Lorean's arrest was imminent. The government, who had now had enough, instructed Sir Kenneth Cork to shut up shop. Cork, unaware of the developments in California, was desperate for one last attempt to save the factory and its jobs. He wired De Lorean and told him that if he could come up with $20 million by 20 October, DMC might be saved from total bankruptcy. De Lorean wired back that this was possible.

On 18 October, Hetrick flew into Los

Below: ***Lord Goodman, the lawyer who issued a series of libel writs on behalf of John De Lorean.***

Below Left: ***William Morgan Hetrick, who was charged with De Lorean.***

Left: ***De Lorean walks out of prison, ten days after his arrest, following posting of a $10 million bail bond.***

Angeles with the cocaine. Hours later he was arrested in a Hollywood restaurant and shipped off to the Federal Penitentiary at Terminal Island.

The following afternoon, oblivious to Hetrick's fate, John De Lorean flew from New York to Los Angeles. Hoffman picked up De Lorean at Los Angeles airport and drove him to the Sheraton La Reina Hotel. Video cameras recorded everything as they entered room 501 and were greeted by 'Mr Vicenza'.

Vicenza pulled a suitcase out of a wardrobe and opened it. It was full of small packages and he handed one of them to De Lorean. De Lorean hefted it in his hand and said: 'This is as good as gold, and just in the nick of time.'

Champagne was being passed round the room when a stranger burst in. 'Hi, John,' he said. Jerry West, with the FBI. You're under arrest for narcotics violations.' There was a long silence as West put the handcuffs on De Lorean. Finally he spoke. 'You've got the wrong man,' he said.

De Lorean spent the next ten days at the Federal Penitentiary at Terminal Island. Bail was finally set at $10 million. John De Lorean was facing a possible jail sentence of seventy-two years and he wasn't taking any chances. He retained California's top criminal lawyer, Howard Weitzman, to conduct his defence.

The trial lasted almost three months and was a jamboree. Weitzman's defence was based on his contention that De Lorean had been 'entrapped' – that is to say he was seduced by the FBI into an illegal act, which he would not have considered without their active encouragement. Weitzman also set about discrediting Hoffman and the other prosecution witnesses whom he portrayed as anything from muddled and inconsistent to outright liars. It was a powerful defence.

But there were still those damning tapes, which showed John De Lorean gloating over a suitcase of cocaine and describing it as 'good as gold'.

Weitzman for his part described the FBI as an organization which would go to any lengths to secure a prosecution.

Weitzman's argument won the day and, when the jury filed back into court on 16 August, they returned a verdict of 'Not Guilty' on all five counts.

However John De Lorean's troubles were far from over. The GPD affair would not go away, and investigations on both sides of the Atlantic wanted to know what had happened to the missing $18 million. He has been arrested and acquitted of fraud on two occasions, but civil and criminal cases against him continue to pile up and many of them are still unresolved at the time of writing.

Below: ***Smiles for the press, as De Lorean and his wife Christina Ferrare leave court during hearings in 1984.***